KA 0386745 5

Education, Poverty, Malnutrition and Famine

Also available in the Education as a Humanitarian Response series

Education as a Global Concern, Colin Brock

Education and Minorities, edited by Chris Atkin

Education and HIV/AIDS, edited by Nalini Asha Biggs

Education, Refugees and Asylum Seekers, edited by Lala Demirdjian

Education and Internally Displaced Persons, edited by Christine Smith Ellison
    and Alan Smith

Education, Aid and Aid Agencies, edited by Zuki Karpinska

Education and Disadvantaged Children and Young People, edited by Mitsuko
    Matsumoto

Education and Reconciliation, edited by Julia Paulson

Education and Natural Disasters, edited by David Smawfield

Also available from Bloomsbury:

Education around the World: A Comparative Introduction, Colin Brock and
    Nafsika Alexiadou

*Comparative and International Education: An Introduction to Theory, Method
    and Practice (2ⁿᵈ edition)*, David Phillips and Michele Schweisfurth

Education, Poverty, Malnutrition and Famine

Education as a Humanitarian Response

Edited by

Lorraine Pe Symaco

UNIVERSITY OF WINCHESTER
LIBRARY

B L O O M S B U R Y

LONDON • NEW DELHI • NEW YORK • SYDNEY

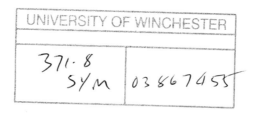

UNIVERSITY OF WINCHESTER

371.8
SYM   03867455

Bloomsbury Academic
An imprint of Bloomsbury Publishing Plc

50 Bedford Square   1385 Broadway
London   New York
WC1B 3DP   NY 10018
UK   USA

www.bloomsbury.com

Bloomsbury is a registered trade mark of Bloomsbury Publishing Plc

First published 2014

© Lorraine Pe Symaco and Contributors, 2014

Lorraine Pe Symaco has asserted her right under the Copyright, Designs and Patents Act, 1988, to be identified as Volume Editor of this work.

All rights reserved. No part of this publication may be reproduced or transmitted in any form or by any means, electronic or mechanical, including photocopying, recording, or any information storage or retrieval system, without prior permission in writing from the publishers.

No responsibility for loss caused to any individual or organization acting on or refraining from action as a result of the material in this publication can be accepted by Bloomsbury or the editor.

British Library Cataloguing-in-Publication Data
A catalogue record for this book is available from the British Library.

ISBN: HB: 978-1-4725-1158-4
     PB: 978-1-4725-0910-9
     ePDF: 978-1-4725-1269-7
     ePub: 978-1-4725-1211-6

Library of Congress Cataloging-in-Publication Data
Education, poverty, malnutrition and famine / edited by Lorraine Pe Symaco.
pages cm. – (Education as a humanitarian response)
Includes bibliographical references.
ISBN 978-1-4725-1158-4 (hardback) – ISBN 978-1-4725-0910-9 (paperback)
1. Poor–Education–Case studies. 2. Malnutrition in children–Case studies.
3. Humanitarian assistance–Case studies. I. Symaco, Lorraine Pe, 1978–

LC4065.E38 2014
371.826′94–dc23

2013045200

Typeset by Integra Software Services Pvt. Ltd.
Printed and bound in India

Contents

Notes on Contributors

Nalini Asha Biggs is a doctoral student in the Department of Communication, University of California, San Diego, US with a B.A. from the same university, an M.A. in Special Education from San Diego State University, US an M.Ed. in International Education from the University of Sydney, Australia and an M.Litt. in Education from the University of Oxford, UK. Her research explores how disability is constructed within educational institutions and activities with a focus on the attitudes and beliefs of educational professionals.

Guillaume Charvon studied Philosophy at Paris-Sorbonne University, France. He has been a full-time Fourth World volunteer since 2003. He later became director of ATD Fourth World in Burkina Faso (West Africa) for six years. He has been based in Boston, USA, since September 2013 for the purpose of continuing a dialogue between ATD Fourth World and the world of academic research.

Elaine Chase is a Research Officer at the Oxford Institute of Social Policy, University of Oxford, UK. Her research interests include the sociological dimensions of poverty, migration, social exclusion, rights and well-being. She has conducted research and written widely on these themes from a UK and international perspective and with a particular focus on children, young people and communities most likely to face marginalization and disadvantage.

Rys Farthing is currently completing her DPhil in the Department of Social Policy at the University of Oxford, UK. Her current work focuses on exploring the capacity for participatory policy work with children and young people from socio-economically deprived backgrounds in developed nations. She has previously worked in universities and NGOs, in both England and Australia, exploring young people's politics and participation.

Yael Freimann's research focuses on food security issues in the Northeast United States. She holds an MSc in Sustainable Development from the School of Oriental and African Studies, University of London, UK, and is affiliated with the Centre for Development, Environment, and Policy (CEDEP), University of London, UK. She recently completed a study on the effectiveness of food pantries on alleviating food insecurity in Hartford, Connecticut.

Anupama Hazarika is a Medical Doctor and Public Health Specialist, with experience of implementing national programmes in some of the toughest terrains of India, having worked at the state, regional and national levels. Currently, Anupama works as a Senior Consultant for Policy and Coordination at the National Health Systems Resource Centre, where she is involved in providing technical assistance for policy, planning, and monitoring the National Rural Health Mission to the Ministry of Health, Government of India.

Roderick Hicks is an Education Consultant with over 30 years' experience in developing countries, strengthening education within fragile states and those emerging from conflict. He has worked within ministries of education, United Nations agencies and non-governmental organizations where he has led significant and complex projects and programmes. He has been involved in education development in Somalia, Malawi, Southern Sudan, Ethiopia, Eritrea, Kenya and Uganda and is especially concerned with issues of language policy and curriculum development.

Altaf Hossain is a Research Fellow and Team Leader in the Research and Development Unit of the Institute of Educational Development–BRAC University (IED-BRACU). He was part of a team that designed, planned and implemented a large community and school survey for Consortium for Research on Educational Access, Transitions and Equity (CREATE) in Bangladesh. He has also written several research monographs for CREATE. He is currently completing his doctorate in education from the University of Sussex, UK.

Naoko Imoto has been coordinating the emergency response of around 200 organizations for the education sector in Haiti as deputy cluster coordinator as well as the information manager after the earthquake in 2010. She also served as an education officer in UNICEF, Sri Lanka, during the height of the civil war. Prior to joining UNICEF, she worked in various education and other projects in Rwanda, Sierra Leone, Kenya and Ghana.

Helena Murseli served as education manager in Haiti, working on aspects related to access and learning opportunities for the most vulnerable in the aftermath of the 2010 earthquake. Helena has worked in the education sector of various organizations in several countries and regions including the Balkans and Eastern Europe, Western Africa, Afghanistan and Haiti. Helena holds two master's degrees in education from Paris Descartes University, France and the Institutions for Research in Sociology and Economics of Education (IREDU), University of Bourgogne, France.

T. Sundararaman is currently Executive Director of National Health Systems Resource Centre, the apex technical support institution to the National Rural Health Mission, Government of India. From 2002 to 2007, he headed the State Health Systems Resource Centre, Chhattisgarh, and prior to this was a Professor, Internal Medicine, at the Jawaharlal Institute of Postgraduate Medical Education and Research, India.

Lorraine Pe Symaco is Director of the Centre for Research in International and Comparative Education (CRICE) at the University of Malaya, Malaysia. She holds a DPhil in Education from the University of Oxford. Lorraine is editor of the *Journal of International and Comparative Education* (*JICE*) and *Education in South East Asia* (Bloomsbury, 2013), and co-edits the series *Education in the Asia Pacific Region: Issues, Challenges and Prospects* (Springer).

Benjamin Zeitlyn is a Lecturer in International Education and Development at the University of Sussex. He works mainly on access to education in areas such as policies for children who drop out of school and assessing the impact of private provision of education. At the Sussex Centre for Migration Research he worked on transnational childhoods and identities, principally with British Bangladeshi children. He is the 'qualitative theme leader' in the Migrating out of Poverty Consortium, which is a 7 year international research programme on migration and development.

Series Editor's Preface

Colin Brock

Underlying this entire series on *Education as a Humanitarian Response* is the well-known adage in education that 'if we get it right for those most in need we will likely get it right for all if we take the same approach'. That sentiment was born in relation to those with special educational needs within a full mainstream system of schooling.

In relation to this series, it is taken further to embrace not only the special educational needs of those experiencing disasters and their aftermath, whether natural or human-made, but also to other groups who may be significantly disadvantaged. Indeed, much can be learned of value to the provision of mainstream systems from the holistic approach that necessarily follows in response to situations of disaster. Sadly, very little of this potential value is actually perceived, and even less is embraced.

Consequently, one of the aims of the series, both in the core volume *Education as a Global Concern* and in the contributing volumes, is to bring the notion of education as a humanitarian response to the mainstream, and those seeking to serve it as teachers, other educators and politicians.

Lorraine Pe Symaco has addressed this fundamental issue both in her valuable overview chapter and in her selection of sub-themes and authors for the contributions that follow. She has been able to show that the issues of poverty, malnutrition and famine act not only independently but sometimes also in concert with education, and that different forms of education can be both negative and positive in relation to addressing the many challenges these issues pose to sustainable development and human survival. This is achieved through a number of well-chosen and argued examples from widely differing locations in less developed countries and regions, as well as timely reminders from the USA and UK. The former in particular shows how malnutrition is not necessarily the result of lack of food but can be the opposite. Obesity in primary school children is a massive and growing problem for schooling in these two countries. Furthermore, the UK has the worst profile of child poverty in Western Europe despite being still in aggregate terms one of the richest nations in the world.

This particular volume, *Education, Poverty, Malnutrition and Famine*, is a valuable and instructive contribution to the series *Education as Humanitarian Response*. I am most grateful to Dr Symaco for constructing and producing such a wide-ranging set of examples and a challenging introductory overview to an issue that will no doubt become even more challenging as the world's total population continues to rise exponentially, as graphically illustrated in Stephen Emmot's graphic book *10 Billion* (2013). This number is the likely global population by the mid-twenty-first century. By 2100, it will likely be 28 billion, and where will poverty, malnutrition and famine be then? Can education help the human species to cope?

These chapters provide some insight into the answer to this question.

Colin Brock
Senior Research Fellow in Comparative
and International Education
University of Oxford, UK

Education, Poverty, Malnutrition and Famine: An Overview

Lorraine Pe Symaco

Chapter Outline

Introduction

Poverty, malnutrition and famine exist in variant degrees in both developing and developed countries. The intricate issues brought forth depend on factors such as, among others, the level of development of a country and its governance, along with concerns inherent to each. The issues figure prominently in the discourse with various studies that allot much space to the interrelated effects of poverty, malnutrition and famine in the overall general well-being of individuals. Global calls to significantly reduce its adverse effects are exemplified for instance through the Millennium Development Goal (MDG) of eradicating extreme poverty and hunger. The role of education in possibly condensing its undesirable influences has led to myriad studies linking the role of education to poverty and the contribution of education and health to the elimination of malnutrition and famine, as well as those analysing education access concerns brought about by poverty, among other things. This book aims to give a global overview of the role of education as a humanitarian response – what it is and how it can be achieved – in relation to the issues at hand. Country case studies from deprived East and West Africa, the thriving economy of India and its neighbour Bangladesh, disaster-prone Haiti and the Philippines to the more developed United Kingdom and the USA will highlight how the utilization of proper education can conceivably help alleviate the effects generated by poverty, malnutrition and famine.

The agenda on poverty alleviation and the role of education

With the 2015 deadline on the horizon, the MDG goal of eradicating extreme poverty and hunger has proven to be one of the major factors in pushing for the elimination of poverty. At the global level, it has been reported that the proportion of people living in extreme poverty has been halved. The number of people living on less than 1.25 US dollars (USD) a day has been reduced to 22 per cent in 2010 as compared to 47 per cent in 1990 (UN 2013). Additionally, improved access to sources of drinking water and with the number of poor urban dwellers in the developing world declining, with over 200 million accessing adequate living spaces, expectations are high. However, 1 out of 8 people continue to be undernourished, 1 out of 6 children under the age of 5 remain underweight, and 1 in 4 are stunted (UN 2013). Quantifying poverty nonetheless is another matter. With the 1.25 USD baseline as extreme poverty, then probably no one from developed countries such as the USA would be considered 'extremely poor'. The 'less than a dollar a day' figure is usually used as the domestic poverty base for countries mainly found in sub-Saharan Africa or South Asia (Besley and Burgess 2003). This would then of course extend to what quantifies as suitable provision for those living in poor countries. Given this, a number of policies ranging from improving health care to enhancing human capital are advanced in line with the desire to reduce poverty on a global scale. Locally, each country has its own initiatives geared towards the development of its population. Education has been central in moves secured by countries in line with the needed advancement. A number of studies have highlighted the need to ensure that the human resources of countries are in tune with the skills required for the rising knowledge-based economy and globalization of services (Mohd Asri and Crossley 2013; Symaco 2012; 2013a; Tsuruta 2013). Conversely, with the upsurge of global integration, global inequalities have also been documented (Pieterse 2002).

Nevertheless, international policy focus has been on poverty alleviation, and unarguably, the human capital approach to development has been one of the more prominent syntheses in literature. Take the case of the global call for Universal Primary Education (UPE), where the expansion of education has been documented inevitably through to the secondary and higher education level, though drop-out rates are still a concern especially for poorer households. Still, the role of education in moderating the effects of poverty has been advanced. Duflo (as cited in Besley and Burgess 2003) found out that for every additional year in schooling in developing countries, there is an increase of 6–10 per cent in earnings, congruent with evidence suggested in developed countries as well (Krueger and Lindhal 2001). On the one hand, the variance of inequality across countries and regions were explored by De Gregorio and Lee (2002) in their study which shows that educational factors, such as attainment and the distribution of education, play a role in income distribution, and that the social expenditure of governments has a positive influence on a more equal income distribution. This role of social expenditure is mainly because it 'consists of direct transfer to the poor, increasing their income and redistributing income from rich to poor [and it] promote[s] access for the poor to education and other human-capital-enhancing activities ... ' (p. 406), while the role of education supports the theoretical premise that 'a higher dispersion of education, given its level, results in high returns to education, and hence generates stronger incentives to invest in education' (p. 408).

Granted the substantial role of education in the poverty-reduction agenda (with poverty also being linked to malnutrition, and famine in some), what role does education have specifically as a 'humanitarian response' in terms of easing the impacts of the three along with the goal of enhancing human development and capabilities? The following sections will review some of the prominent factors and themes discussed in this book as pertaining to the role of education and poverty alleviation.

Education as a humanitarian response

The role of education as a 'humanitarian response' in the context of providing a potential solution to issues such as, in this case, poverty, malnutrition and famine ranges from the likelihood to improve social mobility through enhanced human capacity, to improving one's knowledge base through informal education. It is quite often the case that education has been emphasized as a major drive in keeping with a country's development plans. The supposed ability of education to blur boundaries and bridge gaps in societies has as a result persistently placed this sector as one of the foremost priorities in development agendas worldwide. Education as a humanitarian response has typically been linked with 'education for emergencies'. Clearly, there is a need to provide educational support to people who have suffered from disasters, be they natural, human-made or a combination of both (Brock 2012, p. 13). Brock further emphasizes that a humanitarian response to educational need 'requires it to be appropriate to that need in respect of every individual at any particular time and place. In terms of both an individual and a community – whether it be local, national, global – the need is to assist stability allied to sustainable development' (ibid, p. 13). How then does education play a part in the solution to reduce poverty, malnutrition and famine globally? What are the tangible outputs that the education sector, both in the formal and informal setting, can employ to impact the issues at hand?

Education, disasters and governance

Education plays an important role in mitigating the effects of disasters – human-made or otherwise – through granting proper information to the individuals concerned. Literature has documented studies that point out the relevance of training, whether in formal schooling or through community participation, in preparing for the effects of a disaster. Symaco (2013b) takes note of the young Tilly Smith, who was reminded of a lesson from her geography class about receding waters prior to a tsunami formation, thus saving a number of lives in Thailand during the December 2004 tsunami that claimed hundreds of thousands of others. In the wake of the 2004 tsunami, the Hyogo Framework for Action, 2005–2015, which was adopted at the World Conference for Disaster Reduction (2005), identified education, along with sustainable management and planning, as the only effective long-term solution to prepare for, and alleviate, future tsunamis and other natural disasters (UNESCO 2007 p. ii). This role of education for sustainable development (ESD) as adopted at the 1992 Earth Summit reorients the need for education to develop public awareness, among other things, conceivably under the broad umbrella of issues relating to sustainable development. Cantell and Elias (2009) likewise acknowledge that

ESD should promote education that will foster skills in individuals so that they are able to face new challenges with rational and intelligent advances that can affect their lives.

In this book, Helena Museli and Naoko Imoto discuss the role of education and aid in rebuilding Haiti after the devastating 2010 earthquake that struck the country. The role of humanitarian assistance as providing support in rebuilding the education sector and reducing vulnerability after the earthquake is taken into account. Given the age-based vulnerabilities of disasters, children run the most risk in such events. However, Wachtendorf et al. (2008) describe the chance of children sustaining disaster-resilience, therefore re-emphasizing the need to integrate disaster mitigation courses within the formal school setting, this especially being relevant (but not restricted) to developing countries that run threat to adequately supplying the needed resources should disasters strike. Studies show that over the period 1980–2004, casualties per event were 'higher by orders of magnitude' in low and middle income countries as opposed to high income countries (Bayer et al. 2005). Pertinent to this argument, Murseli and Imoto call for the need to increase and improve access to educational services to the poorest in Haiti to equip children with learning competencies that will enable them to contribute to the overall well-being of their communities. Unfortunately, weak governance in related structural issues, recurrence of emergencies and lack of adequate funding, among other factors, make it difficult to fully implement an ideal and unqualified education system.

On a similar note, the Philippines has been witness to a long-standing conflict in some areas in the south of the country, Mindanao. The struggle between the Philippine government and the MILF and MNLF factions, as explored in the chapter by Lorraine Pe Symaco, recounts how this has led to pushing the Autonomous Region of Muslim Mindanao (ARMM) and the Filipino Muslims farther into poverty. The dire need for access to basic services such as education and health has further relegated the region to be one of the least, if not the least, developed in the country. Regrettably for this region, corruption is rampant, which makes it all the more difficult to address developmental concerns. The creation of a middle class through the expansion of education has been reported to be one of the major detriments to corruption in literature, which also shows that investment in education can be used to alleviate poverty in one way or another (You and Khagram 2005; Paldam 2002). Then again, despite policies initiated by the government to improve social services such as education, Symaco observes that inadequate and weak governance is chronic, further diminishing the prospects of the community to secure employment or to access essential services. On a national scale also, corruption is manifest, which weakens efficient delivery from institutions and makes the poor more vulnerable to extortion. Corruption also promotes inequality when institutions fail to provide qualitative vital services such as education by limiting social mobility among certain groups in the long run. In a democracy such as the Philippines, political equality is 'not sufficient to curb corruption without economic equality, and democratisation in highly unequal societies may even generate increased corruption in the short run' (You and Khagram 2005, p. 155).

Education and health

The interrelated and intricate role of education and health in development has resulted in a number of cases reporting the contribution of health to educational outcomes, and the impact of parental education attainment on health and poverty, among others. Causal pathways between education and health were reported by Blane (as cited in Chandola et al. 2006, p. 338) first through cognitive ability or intelligence in childhood as affecting both educational achievement and adult health outcomes. Since intelligence is believed to predict lower mortality rates for all causes (which can be explained through the ability of individuals to interpret health education messages well, thus ensuring better response in relevant cases) (Gottfredson and Deary 2004). Second, childhood socio-economic circumstance is also said to affect both education and health outcomes. This stems possibly from the effect of parental social class on educational and health attainments. Lower parental social class is said to contribute more to earlier adult morbidity, while a higher social class supports further interest in a child's education, thereby increasing educational attainment and perchance improving health outcomes at the same time. Similarly, adult socio-economic circumstances affect both education and health since 'higher education leads to higher occupational class and income, which, in turn, increases the chance of better health' (p. 340). It is clear then how this predisposes people in poverty to health problems that can otherwise be avoided when given proper education. Blane also reported that the state of health in childhood and adolescence affects a child's educational attainment. Inevitably, poor health leads to limited educational attainment of children through possible drop-out concerns and other related issues already discussed, thereby increasing other health problems.

In this book, the interrelated roles of educational access and exclusion, and poverty and health in Bangladesh are examined by Benjamin Zeitlyn and Altaf Hossain. They use indicators of access to education through zones of exclusion defined through (a) access to preschool; (b) levels of children never enrolled; (c) children who drop out of school and; (d) children who are at risk of exclusion or those 'silently excluded'. In their study, Zeitlyn and Hossain found clear links between poverty and exclusion from schools since children from poorer households are more likely to drop out of school or not attend school at all. Indicators of poverty such as poor health/nutrition also reveal substandard educational outcomes. By raising awareness between poverty-related education exclusion and health issues, the authors signified that problems associated with these can be avoided. And as Gottfredson and Deary (2004) point out, the inequality in social structure, and believably education, is one of the more central reasons why research makes the connection between higher IQ and better health.

The effect of inequality on health is also documented by Sundararaman and Anupama, with reference to India. In their chapter, they discuss parental education as one of the factors affecting poverty level. For instance, Sundararaman and Anupama show us that higher literacy rates positively correlate with the decline in malnutrition and child mortality. They also highlight the need to invest in education that can reasonably reduce poverty. The variables of inequality brought forth by lack of access to education make it all the more practical to invest in education, broadly defined. Ross and Wu (1995) highlight the link of inequality to health and take into account work and economic conditions and socio-psychological factors as relevant to the issue at hand. Ross and Wu maintain that, first, well-educated people are less likely to be unemployed, thus favouring a better economic condition overall, and that, second, well-educated people are more likely to have stronger social support in addition to their existing (economic) resources. Given this logic, it follows that education helps an individual to rise in his/her economic status and, as a result, improve his/her general health condition.

Education and the grassroots approach

Africa continues to be one of the most deprived regions in the world. Perhaps the region is one of the first to come to mind when one is tasked to identify places where poverty, malnutrition and famine acutely exist. Fittingly so, since extreme poverty and low access to social services are documented in the region, along with ominous concerns such as the HIV/AIDS pandemic. Two chapters in this book focus on the pivotal role of education in the alleviation of poverty, malnutrition and famine in sub-Saharan Africa. Guillaume Charvon and Elaine Chase examine the meaning of 'Education for All' for people living in extreme poverty in Burkina Faso, while Roderick Hicks examines the causal links of education with poverty alleviation in East Africa. Aside from the proposed solution that the education sector seemingly suggests in relation to poverty alleviation in this region, one prominent theme arising from both chapters is the importance of incorporating grassroots perspectives in education policy and re-orientations. In a region that begets and depends centrally on aid, this is a valid concern that needs to be addressed. It should be noted that sub-Saharan Africa as a whole is witness to governments and institutions that focus on nation-rebuilding and unremittingly tackling financial concerns that take the emphasis away from the need to integrate and use policies that manifest indigenous knowledge, needs and priorities (Corkery et al. 1995). The Freedom of the World 2013 reports significant advances in freedom and democracy in sub-Saharan Africa, and with the marked African pro-democracy drives developing – akin to and imaginably encouraged by the Arab Spring – it is clear that a multiparty democracy is gaining ground (Freedom House 2013; The Economist 2011). Suitably then, as underlined by Besley and Burgess (2003), the fundamental principle of a 'representative democracy' is to give voice to people, subject to policy, in making policy.

Who, then, are the individuals concerned in policy making? The existence of participants in every organizational dimension or community has led to the use of the 'stakeholder' concept as a framework for various systems and societal topics (Buchholz and Rosenthal 2004; Jawahar and Mclaughlin 2001; Phillips and Reichart 2000). Freeman's (1984) work has further elevated the use of the stakeholder concept in literature. The stakeholder theory in business derives from the idea of how stakeholders significantly influence the policies of an organization, thereby underscoring the importance of maintaining a close relationship between stakeholders and management/organization. If we amend this further and somehow strictly in our definition of 'stakeholder' we refer to local communities in question and by 'management/organization' we mean policy makers, then we alter 'stakeholders' as described by Freeman (1984,: p. 46) as '[the local community] who can affect or is affected by the achievement of the [relevant policy maker's] objective'. There is also the seeming importance of addressing the expectations of 'stakeholders' in any setting. The conceptualization of this theory is similar to the *stakeholder model* and relating this to education policy and their receivers, ideally, is a plan in which the focal organization of policies is the 'hub of the wheel' with the stakeholder/local community 'at the ends of the spoke of the wheel' (Frooman 1999:p. 191). Applicable to this model, a dyadic approach is maintained through explaining the influence of an individual 'stakeholder' and the independent relationships that are mostly focused on the organization's or a certain policy's vantage point.

Charvon and Chase in their chapter discuss findings of an action research project which illuminates the educational challenges of a transitional society like Burkina Faso. The perspective of people living in extreme poverty and the seeming discrepancy between the realities faced by people in such a situation and the ideals presented to children in school are explored. The divergent perspectives arise ostensibly from the different knowledge structures inherent to each. Chavron and Chase further recount how there is an apparent need to strike a balance between the two divergent value systems of urbanization – typifying modernisms, and the rural life, which is sturdily linked to community and traditions. Further, they emphasize that an education system that is made relevant and appropriate in the context in which it is implemented, and one that takes into account the local knowledge base available, is vital in order to ensure the expected realizations of the system.

The chapter on East Africa by Roderick Hicks explores the impact of education on poverty alleviation, on the one hand, and of poverty on educational achievement, on the other. Providing illustrative examples from Uganda, Somalia and Kenya, among others, Hicks explains the need to provide a school-based curriculum that is able to respond to the modern economy and at the same time made relevant to the local community. He also emphasized the need to ensure that basic skills are taught early on to guarantee essential life skills in the long run. Addressing current bottlenecks in the system as well as assessing the probable negative impacts of certain educational interventions on the local community is also advocated in the chapter in order to optimise the effects of education for everyone. And as Corkery et al. (1995, p. 9) fittingly suggest

> (…) (a) society is not a passive element in policy-making. Its members (farmers, workers, industrialists, parents, teachers, either individually or in groups and associations) have vested interests in the outcomes of the process of national policy formulation. It includes all those people and institutions who assume, based on their expertise and specialist knowledge, the significance the policy will have for them (…)

Education and inequality

The education experiences of people from deprived communities are often different from that of those coming from well-to-do households. For one, people from poorer households struggle to make ends meet and additionally ensure that they have enough resources to provide for their children's 'add-on' needs in school (e.g. uniforms, books and stationeries), if they have the ability to actually send their children to schools. A number of governments have advocated the implementation of feeding programmes in schools through, as the chapters in the book will show, school gardens, meal vouchers and so on. Policy initiatives aimed at improving the educational attainments and health outcomes of the vulnerable (especially children) are often observed in developing countries (Afridi 2010). However, as aforementioned, cases of poverty and malnutrition are not confined to developing countries alone. In this book, two chapters are devoted to deliberating the role of education in reducing the effects of poverty and malnutrition in the UK and the USA.

The educational marginalization experienced by children from deprived communities across England is explored by Rys Farthing, particularly linking hunger and educational achievement. Among the financially disadvantaged students, missing out on school trips and skipping meals to avoid embarrassment (of having to present their 'meal vouchers') as a result of peer pressure are but just some of the concerns discussed in the chapter. While very few children are in actuality excluded from mainstream education in the UK, discrepancies within the system itself are manifest. In literature, Ladd (2002) shows the positive correlation between the socio-economic composition of the school and its performance. Schools with a majority of disadvantaged children exhibited weaker gains in test scores in contrast to stronger gains for schools which have more affluent students. The latter can be explained by the positive spill-over effects of one student to the next, availability of resources and the presence of better qualified teachers. Comparably, though there is no proven connection demonstrated by Farthing, the chapter quantifies how students from less-advantaged groups are not treated well by their teachers, which might explain the frequent cutting of classes by such students.

The notion of inequality is further discussed by Nalini Asha Biggs and Yael Freimann in their chapter on the USA. Issues dealing with food insecurity and nutrition are discussed. The epidemic of obesity as affecting the country and how this form of malnutrition affects the general well-being in the long term; the reliance of a significant number of Americans on emergency food supplies; and the promising development of school gardens are highlighted in their chapter. They also highlight that many of the indicators of low income can be considered an indicator of food insecurity. Studies show us that on-site feeding programmes in schools have been seen to increase likely benefits for its recipients (Afridi 2010; Jacoby 2002), similar to the impact of school gardens in California (i.e. in terms of improving the nutritional intake of students) as demonstrated by Biggs and Freimann. When applied to developing countries especially, on-site feeding programmes have a positive impact on improving school enrolment and daily attendance. Research suggest that feeding programmes can improve the cognitive abilities of their receivers and given that better learning can render higher earnings, such programmes can have a significant impact on poverty reduction (Afridi 2010; Rose and Dyer 2008).

Closing remarks

We have illuminated here the issues of poverty, malnutrition and famine, and how education as a 'humanitarian response' can help alleviate the scale of such challenge. It is vital to consider the inter-related roles of the different sectors such as education, health and governance, among others, to warrant the optimal benefits of proposed interventions. While it is necessary to consider the complex issues of poverty, malnutrition and famine, it is just as necessary to consider the equally complex factors interjecting the prevalence of such. In the chapters to follow, the inequalities brought about by these global concerns will be discussed and interventions will be proposed on how one can optimally utilize the education sector in order for it to achieve its role as a formidable solution to breaking the incessant cycle that is so inherent in poverty.

It is hoped that this book will serve as an invaluable reference on the role of education in the globally pertinent issues of poverty, malnutrition and famine. In this light, I would like to thank all the contributors who have worked hard on this project, for contributing their chapters which explored the unique case country/region studies in relation to an ever-significant theme, truly valuable contributions to the field.

References

Afridi, F. (2010). Child welfare programs and child nutrition: evidence from a mandated school meal program in India. *Journal of Development Economics*, *92*(2), 152–165.

Bayer, J., Mechler, R. and Pflug, G. (2005). Refocusing disaster aid. *Science*, *309*(5737), 1044–1046.

Besley, T. and Burgess, R. (2003). Halving global poverty. *The Journal of Economic Perspectives*, *17*(3), 3–22.

Brock, C. (2012). Perspectives on the contribution of higher education to education as a humanitarian response, *Journal of International and Comparative Education*. Available at: http://crice.um.edu. my/inaugural-issue.html [accessed 4 July 2013].

Buchoolz, R. and Rosenthal, S. (2004). Stakeholder theory and public policy: how governments matter. *Journal of Business Ethics*, *51*(2), 143–153.

Cantell, M. and Elias, D. (2009). For bulls and bears alike: education as an investment in sustainable development. In C. Brock and L.P. Symaco (Eds.) *Education in South East Asia*. Oxford: Symposium Books, 323–340.

Chandola, T., Clarke, P., Morris, J.N. and Blane, D. (2006). Pathways between education and health: a causal modelling approach. *Journal of the Royal Statistical Society, 169*(2), 337–359.

Corkery, J., Land, A. and Bossuyt, J. (1995). The process of policy formulation: institutional path or institutional maze? Available at: http://www.ecdpm.org/Web_ECDPM/Web/Content/Download. nsf/0/ED2FA8DD08900C60C12571180055BE12/$FILE/PMR3E.pdf [accessed 4 July 2013].

De Gregorio, J. and Lee, J.W (2002). Education and income inequality: new evidence from cross-country data. *Review of Income and Wealth, 48*(3), 395–416.

The Economist(2011). It's progress, even if it's patchy. Available at: http://www.economist.com/node/21531010 [accessed 15 July 2013].

Freedom House (2013). Freedom in the world 2013. Available at: http://www.freedomhouse.org/sites/default/files/FIW%202013%20Booklet%20-%20for%20Web_1.pdf [accessed 15 July 2013].

Freeman, R. (1984). *Strategic Management: A Stakeholder Approach*. Boston: Pitman.

Frooman, J. (1999). Stakeholder influence strategies. *Academic of Management Review*, *24*(2), 191–205.

Gottfredson, L. and Deary, I. (2004). Intelligence predicts health and longevity, but why? *Current Directions in Psychological Science*, *13*(1), 1–4.

Jacoby, H. (2002). Is there an intrahousehold flypaper effect? Evidence from a school feeding program. *Economic Journal 112* (476), 196–221.

Jawahar, I. and McLaughlin, G. (2001). Towards a descriptive stakeholder theory: an organisational life cycle approach. *Academy of Management Review*, *26*(2), 397–414.

Krueger, A. and Lindahl, M. (2001). Education for growth: why and for whom? *Journal of Economic Literature*, *39*(4), 1101–1136.

Ladd, H. (2002). School vouchers: a critical review. *The Journal of Economic Perspectives*, *16*(4), 3–24.

Mohd Asri, M.N. and Crossley, M. (2013). Educational innovation and the knowledge society: development and issues of the clusters of excellence initiative in Malaysia, *Asia Pacific Journal of Education*, *33*(2), 156–169.

Paldram, M. (2002). The cross-country pattern of corruption: economics, culture, and the seesaw dynamics. *European Journal of Political Economy 18*(2), 215–240.

Phillips, R. and Reichart, J. (2000). The environment as a stakeholder? A fairness-based approach. *Journal of Business Ethics, 23*(2), 185–197.

Pieterse, J. (2002). Global inequality: Bringing politics back in. *Third World Quarterly, 23*(6), 1023–1046.

Rose, P. and Dyer, C. (2008). Chronic poverty and education: A review of the literature. Available at: http://www.chronicpoverty.org/uploads/publication_files/WP131_Rose_and_Dyer.pdf [accessed 15 July 2013]

Ross, C. and Wu, C.I. (1995). The links between education and health. *American Sociological Review, 60*(5), 719–745.

Symaco, L.P. (2012). Higher education in the Philippines and Malaysia: the learning region in the age of knowledge-based societies. *Journal of International and Comparative Education, 1*(1), 40–51.

—— (2013a). Education in the knowledge-based society: the case of the Philippines. *Asia Pacific Journal of Education, 33*(2), 183–196.

—— (2013b). Geographies of social exclusion: education access in the Philippines. *Comparative Education, 49*(3), 361–373.

Tsuruta, Y. (2013). The knowledge society and the internationalization of Japanese higher education. *Asia Pacific Journal of Education, 33*(2), 140–155.

UNESCO (2007). *Natural Disaster Preparedness and Education for Sustainable Development*. Bangkok: UNESCO.

United Nations (UN) (2013). *The Millennium Development Goals Report 2013*. New York: NY.

Wachtendorf, T., Brown, B. and Nickle, M. (2008). Big Bird, disaster masters, and high school students taking charge: the social capacities of children in disaster education. *Children, Youth and Environments, 18*(1), 456–461.

You, J.S. and Khagram, S. (2005). A comparative study of inequality and corruption. *American Sociological Review, 70*(1), 136–157.

Education and Poverty Alleviation in Eastern Africa – The Causal Links

1

Roderick Hicks

Chapter Outline

Poverty – what are we measuring?

Whereas education is a wide enough concept not to need any definition, the term 'poverty' does, as it is important to clarify how poverty is measured. In simplistic terms, poverty is normally a measure of income or per capita gross domestic product (GDP). However, some allowances need to be made for 'hidden' income, for example income resultant from subsistence agriculture or where a person carries out his own repairs and maintenance rather than employing someone else. In many areas of East Africa, teachers and health workers are seen as poorly paid, with incomes as low as a 150 US dollars (USD) a month (Goldsmith 2009). However, that same teacher may be given a house or may have a shamba (large garden) and in fact produce most of the food his or her family needs. Thus, when looking at poverty levels and the impact of education we need to look both at the primary income and at the subsidiary incomes that may not be in money terms but can still be enhanced through education. The low income earners who, in school, have learnt how to grow food more effectively, how to mend clothes or their electrical appliances and how to maintain the family in a more healthy way will be well above the poverty level that an income of 150 USD suggests. In fact, many teachers in the rural areas see their salaries as earnings for school fees and luxuries rather than essentials.

Therefore, we need to consider the impact of education on poverty alleviation in wider terms than just impact on the primary income. A fuller definition of poverty would also need to take account of the complex social and psychological factors including welfare and personal esteem as well as a person's relative poverty. Education, which is meant to be an equalizer, may reduce absolute poverty in a society, but, especially where there is a vibrant private education system, may increase inequalities resulting in greater relative poverty and a greater sense of 'being poor' for those in low-income groups. This can come about as the wealthier families send their children to prestigious private or semi-private schools where they get a superior education and create networks for future employment with access to the elite, while lower income families are forced to send their children to the government schools. Government schools may well be improving but not at as fast a rate as the private and prestigious schools.

This duality in an expanding education system is very common. Kenya has its 'National Schools' which, though government, have very limited access for ordinary children. A majority of those in government went to schools such as Alliance. Thus, although district schools may be improving, and being educated at such a district school may increase a child's potential earning power and welfare, that child will never be able to compete on equal terms with the child from Alliance or Hillcrest. Similar cases exist with schools in Uganda (Budo College), Somaliland (Amoud High School) and Ethiopia (Wingate School before the revolution). The majority of top government and business leaders in these countries, irrespective of their political loyalties, will have gone to these schools. Thus, improving and expanding education in the 1960s and 1970s, led to increasing disparities in opportunities and, although absolute poverty declined in terms of GDP, which was growing at over 4 per cent and often as high as 8 per cent (UNCTAD 2001) throughout this period, relative poverty increased dramatically.

The only country to have escaped this pattern was Tanzania, which attempted to block the development of private education in the 1970s and 1980s. Under the strong ideology and direction set by 'Education for Self Reliance' (Nyerere 1967), all schools were under some government control and far greater emphasis was placed on equality and elimination of tribalism, including busing college students from one region to board in a training college in another region to ensure that no college became a 'tribal ghetto', and trying to block people, particularly the wealthier Tanzanians, from sending their children to private schools. This policy may have avoided the worst inequalities associated with its neighbours but it may also have resulted in a decline in overall education standards – or at very least a failure to reach the higher standards of its neighbours' top schools. Tanzania did, however, also avoid having any famines throughout the periods of 1970–1995, a period when some of the worst famines were recorded in Eastern Africa.

Famine as the extreme case

There are many causes of famine and many different definitions of the process that leads to a famine. However, in all cases, famine includes a specific percentage of people who suffer severe malnutrition and starvation. The effects are particularly damaging for young children as they are likely to be handicapped in later life. Research shows that critical brain development occurs from pregnancy to age three and quality early childhood development is a key to ensuring that children enter primary school ready to acquire literacy and numeracy skills. Thus, the negative impact of famine on learning is clear, direct and has been explored elsewhere, for example Thurow's (2012) description of the effect on children's ability to learn concepts if they were malnourished during the Ethiopian famine and statements on the interrelationship between famine and intellectual development (Brookings Institute 2011). This article will only look at the issue of famine in so far as it results from the failure to address poverty alleviation, which in turn leads to communities becoming increasingly vulnerable to other external factors (drought, war, floods, disease), and in so far as education, in the right context, can reduce that vulnerability and provide a community with the strategies for coping with famine or potential famine.

Education leads to eradication of poverty: An assumption

For the last 50 years, donors, non-governmental organizations (NGOs) and governments believed that education, especially basic education, was the one factor that could lead to improvements in welfare and living standards and could end poverty. This link was seen as axiomatic, and a justification for large aid programmes targeting education in low-income countries. For instance, in launching a 60 million USD USAID programme, President Bush declared that the education of children in developing countries 'is key to future economic growth and lasting democracy' (White House Press Release June 2002). Evidence for this link has been produced by World Bank and NGOs though much of the most positive evidence came from South East Asia (World Bank 1990).

A good example of attempts to measure the impact of education on poverty alleviation is put forward by Psacharopulos (1985), who used what was termed a 'Mincerian Wage Equation' as a mathematical model to show the positive impact that education had on earnings and, therefore, poverty reduction. His conclusions stated that the rates of return from education are greatest in (a) the least developed countries; (b) where the focus is on girls' education rather than boys', and (c) where the focus is on primary education rather than higher levels.

In the last ten years, educationalists involved with development have questioned some of these findings. In particular, more recent studies have shown the links between higher education and economic development as being more significant than previously suggested and thus argued that secondary and higher education may be equally or even more cost effective than primary education (Barro 1995), but such revisions still support the cost-effectiveness of investment in education.

Thus, while circumstantial and statistical evidence of the cost-effectiveness of education is strong and welcomed by educationalists themselves, the actual casual link was never particularly well explained and whether all education had a positive impact or only some types of education was never fully discussed nor were the potential negative effects examined.

In fact, suggesting that a negative impact was possible was seen as almost heretical. The belief in the value of education as the mantra to eliminate poverty has been the driving force behind the thinking that has pushed the development agenda. It included such policy sound bites as:

a. Free and Universal Primary Education (UPE) for all.
b. Africa to be free of poverty in 50 years.
c. First build the infrastructure for education, i.e. classrooms and furniture, and the rest will follow.
d. Educate a woman and you educate the family – (thus the emphasis on the gender equality as a means as well as an end).

As already stated, the causal links justifying these sound bites were never properly explored and the success of different aid projects tended to be self-fulfilling. For example, a programme's indicator of success could be the number of learning spaces created or the number of children enrolled in schools rather than the impact this had on welfare and development. The number of girls in schools was frequently used as a key indicator of success in many projects and therefore recent projects supporting secondary education in Somalia specifically used gender enrolment as a key indicator of success. Between 2005 and 2010 the percentage of girls in secondary education rose from 25 per cent to 35 per cent – a clear success (Nkata 2011). In addition, the numbers entering post-secondary institutions almost doubled. However, what these success indicators did not show was whether such increases also represented quality increases that would lead to economic development. Initially in fact, the opposite was true as many girls graduated from secondary schools with 'E' grades in their leaving exams, and, under pressure to deliver on the indicators, some universities allowed girls to enter their first year with 'D' or 'E' grade rather than the 'C' grade specified for boys (Raynor 2009). This in turn led to dropout, frustration and a reinforcement of the negative profiling of women as underperformers academically.

The belief that spending more on education will lead to growth and higher incomes is based on a number of assumptions that do not always hold true. First, it assumes that education actually leads to learning. While one wishes this were always true, recent evidence from UWEZO (2012) and Early Grade Reading Assessments (EGRA) reports suggests that much of basic education is not leading to appropriate learning. Recent studies, such as those in Uganda and Tanzania on Grade two children, suggested that under 10 per cent were actually able to read (Gove & Wetterberg 2011). A similar study, Measuring

Learning Achievements (MLA) at grade four level, still showed that, though not as disastrous, approximately 25 per cent of children remained illiterate after four years. Similar studies in Somalia on grade four and grade seven children carried out by the author have come to similar conclusions. In grade seven, as many as 20 per cent of children were unable to read and 35 per cent were virtually innumerate, for example, 45 per cent were unable to rank numbers by place value (Africa Educational Trust 2011).

Second, it assumes that the learning that does take place will be relevant to economic or social welfare. Curricula used in government and private schools tend to be dictated by the traditional emphasis on content rather than any attempt to look at market needs. Academic, vocational and non-formal education courses offered may be dictated by short-term gain rather than long-term benefits. Thus, the most populous courses in Eastern Africa Universities are in Business Studies. They may be useful but when 70 per cent of graduates are studying business, as happens in Somalia (Nkata 2011), it can hardly lead to growth in key areas of health or technology, especially when the courses omit crucial areas such as the use of spreadsheets. Per capita costs of Business Studies courses are of course much lower than a similar course in civil engineering or other technical, but much-needed, skills. Similarly, vocational education courses have tended to focus on hairdressing and tailoring rather than mechanics or electrical engineering for the same reasons of unit costs rather than market demands.

Lastly, even where learning is both effective and leads to improved productivity it will not necessarily lead to better wealth within the community. Frequently, this is frustrated because the most productive individuals leave their communities to work where salaries are already high. This is common in pastoralist communities of the Horn of Africa. In a recent study, it was found that those with the best learning outcomes were also those that left the communities (Hicks and Hussain, forthcoming). Thus, while the individual may improve his or her earning powers, this may not lead to economic development in the community and, thus, may not be seen as value for money by them.

As a result of education being seen as the mantra for development and poverty eradication, and under pressure from donors, specified success indicators have been achieved. In contrast to these indicators of success, clear negative impacts can also be shown to have followed the policies of expansion in East Africa, as illustrated in the next section, and the relationship is far more complex than these indicators imply. I do not wish to argue that education has no impact on poverty alleviation, only that the casual relation is more complex than usually assumed and thus a more nuanced approach to supporting education is essential.

The relationship between education and poverty

Box A	Box B
Education has a **negative impact** on poverty alleviation	Education has a **positive impact** on poverty alleviation
Box C	**Box D**
Poverty has a **positive impact** on educational achievements	Poverty has a **negative impact** on educational achievements

When education has a negative impact on poverty alleviation (Box A)

In Eastern Africa the drive to universal education has not led to increased wealth across the community nor is its impact on poverty reduction demonstrable in any areas. East African economies expanded rapidly in the 1960s and 1970s but fell back in the mid-1980s and 1990s along with world economic trends (NESC 2013). However, even in times of expansion, there was little real impact on the poverty of the majority. The most demonstrable effects of these drives to expand education in East Africa are described below:

a. UPE in Uganda (2000), Kenya (2003) and Tanzania (1978) led to a decline in the quality of education in order to achieve quantity. This lowering of quality is demonstrable at all levels and led to many graduates being unemployable (Uganda National Exams Board findings reported by Acana 2006; Gove & Wetterberg 2011 and UWEZO 2012). In addition, class sizes expanded dramatically, increasing from 50 to 150 or more in many areas, as observed by the author in Ethiopia Secondary Schools in Addis Ababa, and Ugandan Primary Schools in Gulu and Iganga, amongst others.

b. Rapid dropout between primary 1 and primary 7. In Uganda 71 per cent of children who entered primary 1 dropped out before reaching primary 7, which is approximately 1 million children. (New Vision 2012)

c. A boom in private education, especially low-cost private education, has taken place. In fact this may be the most beneficial, though unexpected, effect of UPE and the nearest to a positive impact on education. However, even here, warning must be given. There is no one model that will work for all areas of East Africa. Successful '$1 a day' schools in Kibera are using a very different model to the small low-cost schools in rural areas of Western Kenya and Eastern Uganda, as evidenced from my discussions with several school head teachers.

What is now emerging is that education in itself, when measured in quantitative terms, is not sufficient to ensure a move away from poverty. In many cases, increases in the quantity of education lead to an increase in poverty, especially relative poverty. The negative causal link between education and poverty can be explained as a result of four key factors. First, the cost of schooling (even nominally free schooling) forces subsistence families into the cash economy in order to find money for fees. Asayo (2011) studied the effects of abolishing secondary school fees in Kenya and showed that the cost of secondary school education remained out of the reach of most poor families. Although the fees were free, the 'non-discretionary' costs of school, such as uniforms, books and stationery were in fact greater than the fees. Thus, the poor either had to find ways of raising cash in the formal economy or their children could not go to secondary school. The need for school fees leads to such families embarking on non-traditional practices that have short-term cash benefits necessary to fund children in school but cause long-term environmental or social and cultural damage, which includes such practices as clearing forest areas and wetlands for formal farming, charcoal burning, selling key animals, and illicit alcohol brewing. All these activities among the poorest families have the primary purpose of generating cash to pay for school fees.

Second, young labour (ages 12–25) is taken away from the family at key times such as planting and harvests or when families need to move pastures, thus reducing the family's subsistence capacity. Asayo's (2011) study showed that a majority of those who did take advantage of 'free' secondary education had been working on their family farmland the year before. This reconfirms the suggestion above that expanding education takes young labour out of the subsistence economy. In addition, as a result of the above factors and because of the direct impact on attitudes of children in school, traditional lifestyles are frequently threatened. Pastoralists, subsistence farmers and traditional fishermen (Hicks et al. 2009) showed how environmental quality declined with increasing levels of development before increasing again, and also the changing attitudes of those being schooled, who no longer wish to follow the old ways. As Kratli (2001) notes, 'most education provision as it is conceived … creates a threat to the livelihood of the pastoralist household' (p. 7). This is of course both a positive force and a negative force for change.

Another aspect is that key areas of environmental controls managed through traditional methods break down, leading to the impoverishment of the environment as land is cleared, traditional methods of farming changed and respect for the value of the environment declines (e.g. fishing along the East African coast, impact of fertilizers, deforestation in Northern Kenya and the Horn). And lastly, levels of inequality increase, leading to increased potential for conflict due to unequal distribution of opportunities and of rewards. This is partly fuelled by high- and medium-cost private education and the inequalities between countries and within countries. In Kenya, the gap between the examination results for Central province and Nairobi as against those for North Eastern and Nyanza has grown wider each year – again a cause for instability.

Thus, in many ways, education can lead to an increase in poverty and a destabilization of the society. In order to compensate for these negative factors, it is essential that the design of education for change is clearly targeted at the areas most likely to impact on poverty and welfare, and that the negative impacts that education can have are factored into plans for expansion of education.

Education has a positive impact on poverty alleviation (Box B)

Clearly it is not all negative, and the right education is almost certainly the prerequisite for development across society and therefore for poverty alleviation. Education has clear positive links to improved welfare and reduction in poverty, at the family level, community level and country level. Hawkes and Ugur (2012) reviewed 39 different papers from a range of countries to illustrate with examples where education does have a positive effect on economic development, in general. However, Hanushek and Woesman (2008) argue that education alone is not sufficient to lead to economic growth, the quality of education is what matters and only education which impacts cognitive development is likely to lead to poverty alleviation. Education is at its most effective in alleviating poverty when it focuses on key skills and knowledge.

It is said that improved literacy and life skills can impact the health and welfare at the level of the family. At the most basic levels, educating mothers does have a number of positive impacts on the welfare of the local community, including (a) improved nutrition and health of children; (b) better farming practice; (c) improved barter and simple selling practices, and (d) greater participation in community decision making. Thus, even where there is no monetary increase in family income, their actual welfare may increase as a result of improved health and agriculture practice. This is a crucial justification for non-formal education which does not necessarily lead to formal education. Reports on literacy classes in South Sudan and in Somalia show significant improvements in welfare that are not necessarily captured in monetary terms (Hussein and Hicks, forthcoming).

Additionally, an awareness of one's rights and obligations within a society, including one's role within both the community and the wider society, and awareness of the opportunities for self-improvement and improvement of the wider family are crucial as driving forces for change and democratization as well as for giving individuals choice as to whether they wish to break away from their traditional patterns. Only basic education for both children and adults can hope to achieve the resultant drive for change. Increased family welfare also results in children obtaining jobs in towns and then repatriating funds for parents and relatives in the village. These are particularly illustrated by expansion of solar electricity, phones, improved housing and toilets, improvements that can be observed throughout Western Kenya over the past ten years.

Where short vocational courses that develop business or other immediately marketable skills are linked to micro-grants, they can lead to increases in disposable income and thus poverty alleviation. This has been demonstrated in both Somaliland and South Sudan (Hussein and Hicks, forthcoming). Furthermore, developing key skills for a substantial minority of people in planning, modern technology – especially in the digital age – finance and key sectors of the economy is essential for any modern economy to advance.

Poverty has a positive impact on educational achievements (Box C)

The family's desire to break the cycle of poverty is probably the most important link of all. It is the driving force for many children and for their parents – the almost Darwinian desire that your children will have a better life than you and that you will have a better life than your parents means very high levels of motivation for both parents and children. Any teacher moving from teaching in Europe to teaching in any East African country is always overwhelmed by the commitment of their students to learn, whatever their conditions. With the introduction of universal primary education and the resultant increase in class size, many poor parents opt to continue paying school fees for local private schools even in rural areas, a sure sign of their desire for quality education.

The recognition of the sacrifices made by parents to educate their children, the fact that parents have sold their best cow or part of their farm or that the mother is brewing illicit gin to pay the fees weighs heavily on many children. They feel it essential that they do reward their parents with success and that they do get a good job so that they can support their younger siblings and/or support their parents in old age. The sense of failure where a child is not successful is, of course, the negative impact.

Poverty has a negative impact on educational achievement (Box D)

There is a clear impact of poverty on access to education, on school enrolment and dropout. Parents with very little surplus may quite justifiably decide that the returns from education will not be sufficient to justify the expenses involved (Jimenez and Jeneker 2004). These expenses are both the cost of schooling and the opportunity costs of losing labour. When school leavers remain unemployed and primary children come home after four years of schooling still unable to read, the decision not to send children to school can be seen as ever more rational. Jienez and Patrinos (2008) estimate that the average rate of return for a year's schooling is 10 per cent of the cost of that schooling. This is higher for low-income countries but is declining as education expands. A parent may feel that this sort of return, with the uncertainties of nil return and the long wait before any return is seen, is just not sufficient to justify the risks to the family's security if they are on the poverty line. Thus, poverty will lead to low school enrolments and early dropout of children for quite rational reasons. Somalia, one of the poorest countries in the world, also has one of the lowest enrolment rates at approximately 30 per cent for primary age children (UNICEF 2010). Recently, some projects have tried to address this issue by providing funding in terms of cash transfers to parents in exchange for girls being sent for education. This is being implemented by Save the Children in Kenya and by UNICEF through scholarships for girls in Somalia. However, such compensation, while recognizing the relevance of opportunity costs, may not be sustainable in the long run and may create a dependency.

Poverty has an even greater impact on the quality of education received than it does on access. These effects are well documented and the impact of poverty on performance is not really in dispute. The impact includes:

a. A home environment that makes study difficult, including lack of light, poor furniture and lack of facilities such as paper and pens. Impressive efforts to address these factors have been made in a number of projects in Northern Uganda with the provision of solar lighting to homes. In 2004, the Department for International Development (DFID) supplied young children in Uganda with paper and pencils to try and alleviate this shortage. The immediate and positive impact was large and measurable, especially in terms of improved handwriting and numeracy as well as the ratio of pencils to children. However, within three years of the project, the number of children in class without pencils had returned to the pre-project level (Hicks 2002).

b. Health issues such as malaria and other debilitating diseases related to poverty and malnutrition lead to frequent absenteeism. Schools in Lake Victoria area of Nyanza have particularly high absentee rates, which can be attributed to the high incidence of debilitating diseases related to the lake, including malaria and bilharzia. Lack of food, especially the lack of lunch, means that many children come to school hungry and are absent in the afternoon, or if present are too hungry to learn (SACMEQ 2013).

c. Duties at home limit study time and can also lead to absenteeism. This affects both sexes but girls more than boys. Girls are most affected by tasks such as cooking, housework and looking after younger children. Boys are more affected by looking after animals and both may be involved in seasonal work such as harvesting and planting. The often unexpected impact on a daily basis can be illustrated through a recent exchange between author and head teacher in Arua, Uganda:

> Author: *Why are so few children at school?*
> Head teacher: *Because it is the mango season, of course!*

d. Customs including early marriage, moranism (coming of age practices among the Maasai), female genital mutilation which, though not directly caused by poverty, tend to coincide with poverty and result in children either being absent or dropping out of school. In Dol Dol, a Massai area of Kenya, about 30 per cent of children are absent on every market day, as indicated by my discussions with the community in Dol Dol. In addition, boys drop out of school once they reach the age to be initiated into being a Moran.

e. Poverty at the community and school level leading to overcrowded classrooms, lack of textbooks, class sizes between 100 and 150, poorly motivated or untrained teachers, lack of buildings and furniture leading to class settings in which 150 children sit in a non-permanent classroom (personal observations of author in Uganda, Eritrea and Ethiopia) with no walls and sitting on stones they carried to school, all these factors reduce the effectiveness of learning. Lack of materials, overcrowding, lack of pencils and children using stones as seats are probably more significant reason for failing to be able to read and write than any issues of methodology.

Poverty, education and famine

Poverty and lack of education may not in themselves be a cause of famine. However, a high level of poverty and a low level of education leave a community vulnerable to famine as soon as any third factor comes into play. The common triggers for famine are drought, war, disease or crop infestations. O'Grady (2009) provides a detailed history of famines over many centuries and concludes that in fact there are fewer in the last few decades and those that happen are less devastating than in the past, with relief organizations much better at responding to them and reducing the damage. He does not directly link famine with education, but any review of the famines covered will show that famines happen where there is poverty and lack of education. These two factors mean that a community is far more vulnerable to famine and has fewer strategies for avoiding the more devastating effects or addressing the root causes of famine. The link with poverty is relatively obvious. If a drought leads to the death of your cattle, then, if you are poor, you have no alternatives for food. If a disease wipes out the maize crops, the richer farmer may have alternatives and surpluses but the poorest farmers and the poorest communities have no alternatives.

The link with education may be less obvious. As already stated in the introduction, children in a community ravaged by famine are likely to have lower levels of cognitive development that will impact their learning. In addition, if famine results in communities moving from one area to another, all the schooling is likely to be disrupted. The recent (2012–2013) famine in Somalia caused massive population displacement. Over 200,000 school-age children were displaced by the famine prior to the opening of schools in September 2012. Many of these had been in school but were faced with losing their schooling as well as their homes as parents took them in search of food or food aid, often gravitating to the outskirts of Mogadishu.

Fortunately, the aid community is now aware of the importance of providing 'Emergency Education'. This can be seen from the response to the famine from a coordination meeting of donors and NGOs:

> Over $20 million will be needed to carry out emergency education plans to help 435,000 children and provide incentives to 5,750 teachers in temporary learning facilities, where food vouchers will also be provided to benefit learners and their families and offer an incentive for children to stay in school, or to enroll for the first time in their lives. (Chorlton 2012)

The above quote does seem to justify O'Grada's (2009) conclusion that the international community's response to famines is now much more effective. Thus, famine can destroy the education of children, but education itself can be a strong defence against famine. There is clear evidence that families and communities with higher levels of education are better equipped to adopt strategies that will defend them, and especially their children, if famine does hit their area. Children whose parents are literate are more likely to survive in a famine than those whose parents are illiterate. Work done by Kiros and Hogan (2001), using figures from the Ethiopian famines in the 1980s, demonstrates this fact. In an area where adult literacy rates were around 14 per cent, the famine was one of the worst in Africa and led to massive relief efforts and public awareness campaigns, worldwide. During the famine, mortality rates stood at 200 per 1000 among children under five. However, where both parents were literate, mortality rates were not as high. They stood at 180 if only the father was literate but improved to 150 if the mother was literate. If the father had a secondary education, then survival rates improved significantly with mortality rates at 114 per 1000 live birth.

If, however, famine is compounded by war, as happened in some areas of Tigre, then the parents' education became insignificant unless the father had post-primary education (Kiros and Hogan 2000). In addition, the parents' education could only help in the short term. If the famine became prolonged in the area then the parents' education became less and less significant to the survival of children. Although the authors do not offer any causal explanations for these links, it would seem likely that education has given the parents the knowledge to ensure better health care and cleanliness, even during the famine and it has provided them with simple problem-solving skills that they can use to develop their own strategies for survival.

Donors, ministries, NGOs and the search for the magic bullet

The response of donors and ministries in East Africa has been to look for single cures that can impact across the whole sector. The pattern has tended to be research that shows up the failings of the system, followed by a single cure that will address this weakness.

As a teacher and then education adviser over the last 40 years, I have been involved in a series of projects that have been influenced by this belief that a single cure will make that crucial difference. I have been part of both the initial research findings and the implementation of the cure. Below I have outlined those trends that have directly impacted my own experiences.

Approximate dates	Evidence of a shortcoming	The cure
1970s	Lack of any technical skills	Investment in technical schools such as those constructed in Somalia and village polytechnics as in Kenya.
1980s	Untrained or badly trained teachers, 35% of teachers untrained in Tanzania with poor English as a key factor inhibiting their teaching	Heavy expenditure on teacher training, mainly pre-service, with buildings and technical assistance such as the DfID projects in Somalia, Tanzania and Kenya with technical assistants referred to as 'KELTS' or Key English Language Teachers
1990/2000	Low enrolment rates and high drop-out rates. Where 70% of children were out of school in Somalia, 35% in Northern Uganda (Educational Statistical Abstracts, Uganda 2009)	Push for free primary education throughout Eastern Africa – in Uganda (2000), Kenya (2002) and Somaliland (2011)
2000 onwards	Gender imbalance in many schools, e.g. areas of North Uganda and Somaliland only 30% enrolment are girls	A variety of projects that focus on girls' education, leading to DfID's Global Funds within Africa
2003/10	Poor teaching which is very teacher-centric with no attempt to involve children in learning	Child-centric methodology and series of short in-service workshops to train teachers in activity-based learning
2008/15	Low literacy and numeracy rates in schools, especially in either first or second language. Low levels of reading ability among school children where EGRA and UWEZO tests show that only 20% of grade three children can decode	New drive to reintroduce mother tongue as the medium of education in grades one and two reading schemes with strong emphasis on the phonics approach – 'Reading for All'.

The criticism of these projects is not that they are misguided in themselves. Far from it, each project was designed in response to research findings and was implemented with considerable professional commitment. The results were also carefully monitored. However, there remained a tendency to oversimplify the problem and look for a single solution to a complex problem. This was followed by a strong advocacy drive to raise awareness of the issue, with research findings to support the solutions. However, such advocacy work tended to label any reservations or alternative solutions as 'outdated' or too 'conservative'. Local concerns that saw wider issues and contextual problems were overlooked. Any alternative approaches were ignored and certainly not funded. Thus, the drive for teacher education in the 1970s overlooked the value of school-based training that was already in existence in an informal way and institutionalized all pre-service training in colleges in the 1970s in countries such as Kenya and Tanzania. However, by the year 2000, complete reversal had taken place and donors were only interested in funding school-based training. Somalia and Somaliland Ministries of Education have been pushing for donor support for a teacher training institute that would be a basis for teacher training from 1999 onwards. The Somalia Delegation of the European Commission, following a report on teacher training, refused to consider any support that was not both in-service and field based with the result that even today, no teacher training college has been established and all training for primary teachers is in-service in Somaliland and Central and Southern Somalia. The exception is Danish International Development Agency (DANIDA), which did provide support to a pre-service college in Garoe and for Secondary Teacher Training in Boroma, but no other donors showed interest.

UPE was one of the Millennium Goals, but in the effort to implement it, the drive became political, the costs and impact on schools were greatly underestimated and local district education officers, who expressed reservations, were ignored or seen as reactionaries. DfID's own assessments of the success of UPE in Uganda were initially far too upbeat and uncritical (Ward et al. 2006). A similar dismissive attitude is now apparent to anyone who questions the value of mother tongue education or suggests an alternative to, or supplement of, pure phonics as the answer to all the reading and, therefore, education problems. This is in spite of many reservations coming from teachers in the field to both policies and puzzlement on the part of the ministries.

A way forward

Can education have a greater impact on poverty alleviation?

The simple answer is *yes*. However, it is easier to criticize existing perceptions and assumptions than to put forward a solution. In fact, I would argue that 'a solution' is one of the problems. We cannot expect to find one solution that will provide high quality education or one solution that will eradicate poverty, not even education, though appropriate education is certainly part of the solution. However, we can follow certain guidelines to try and make education more relevant to improving welfare.

Think small – education made relevant at the community level

If education programmes can be focused at community level, they can have more direct impact on the needs, and eventually the welfare, of that community. Such programmes may not impact the whole country but they will be replicable in similar communities. They need to focus on improving community welfare, not changing the community. This is true whether it be a nomadic, pastoralist, fishing or a farming community. Such programmes should be designed with community input pertaining to what the people of the community really want, how they want to shape their future and what they believe can be effective. It is not necessary that learners join the formal education system unless that is an ambition of the community. It should include key aspects of education that do focus on poverty alleviation and make the community less vulnerable to famine. Adult literacy campaigns, especially for women, health education and effective veterinary and farming skills are examples of aspects of education that can achieve this. Programmes should also look at ways of empowering communities so that they can influence local government regulations and attitudes. Good examples of such programmes include those run in Northern Uganda by a very effective local NGO called Literacy and Basic Education (LABE) and funded by Comic Relief, and those run for pastoral communities in Somalia managed by Africa Educational Trust (AET) and funded by Banyan Tree. Both impact the local communities, strengthening their own capacity to improve community welfare, including literacy and parenting skills. Their impact is described in their end-of-programme external reviews (Hicks 2006).

Think big – appropriate interventions in the formal system

Curriculum made relevant to modern economy

Education planners need to encourage changes in the curriculum and the learning support available so that formal, school-based learning can be more directly linked to the needs of the economy and the local culture. Many curricula in East Africa focus on the traditional content-based subjects, matching the subject areas that have been taught for the last 50 years. Examples of such traditional learning areas are found in the national curriculum for Somalia, Kenya and Uganda, especially at the secondary level. Schools in Somalia still learn about the causes of the First World War and how ox-bow lakes are formed but have little or no exposure to their own history or geography. (Rivers in Northern Somalia are underground for 80 per cent of the year and are unlikely to form the traditional ox-bow). More damaging, few students will have access to knowledge and skills that are crucial for the new technological age. Computer studies are still taught without computers (Kampala International University 2012) – with children learning about computers rather than developing computer skills. The Kenya government has promised a laptop for every child in grade one, but at present few secondary students have access outside Nairobi and even fewer primary teachers know how to use them.

Ensure that basic skills are taught early

It is important to intervene at specific key points of the formal education programmes. In fact, the new emphasis on initial literacy, supported by USAID and World Bank through the Global Partnership for Education Initiative in 2012, could be a crucial step in ensuring that fewer children go through schooling without achieving any value from their education. One can criticize the programme for its apparent unwillingness to look at a range of approaches, but it is clearly focusing at a point where an intervention should be able to make a massive difference. Similar interventions are needed at the same level to target numeracy, an essential pre-vocational skill as well as a life skill. Another focus area may be crucial interventions that will lead to approaches that ensure better cognitive development and problem-solving skills. This could be at several levels.

Tackle the obvious bottlenecks in the education system

There are several obvious bottlenecks in the education system throughout East Africa that only serious money can tackle. The most striking ones include overcrowding, with class sizes of up to 150 and poorly motivated teachers, who have seen their salaries decline in comparison to other professions and lack of infrastructure. The costs of solving these issues are enormous, but it may well be that they are unavoidable if East Africa is to catch up with the better-off countries in terms of Education For All (EFA). If the costs are too great then the policy makers may have to reconsider their priorities and balance the needs of EFA with the needs of a modern economy that needs a significant number of well-trained technical people. Arguably, money spent on training de-motivated teachers on short courses in improved methodology would be more effective if used to raise teachers' salaries to a level that is motivating.

Planning and monitoring programmes

Impact assessment and needs assessment

In any programme planning an educational intervention, it is necessary also to include an assessment of potential negative impacts on local communities, schools and the overall economy (in much the same way as an environmental impact assessment is required on capital projects). This would be a relatively easy policy to adopt, though it would involve a little more preparation and research before an intervention can be approved. An issue of costs arises as, typically, neither an NGO nor a Ministry of Education can afford such preparatory work before it has the money to implement a project, so donors may need to take more responsibility for such research, or be willing to fund local organizations to carry out both needs analysis and impact assessments prior to granting an award.

Provide a variety of responses

To recognize the variety of responses needed if education is to impact welfare is also crucial. The tendency for donors and educationalists to look for a 'silver bullet' should of course be resisted. It is important that planners are free to explore a range of different interventions on a smaller scale and not assume that one approach will lead to development. It is particularly important that local opinions are taken on board and that approaches are modified in the light of local resistance to new ideas.

Conclusion

I hope that in this chapter I have emphasized that the relationship between education, on the one hand, and economic development, poverty and famine, on the other, is not a one-way relationship. It is complex and each impacts the other in both negative and positive ways. Thus, as education clearly has costs to the community, both in terms of opportunity costs and in terms of disruption to the existing society, when any society pushes for education as a way to development, it is taking a risk, especially where that society is fragile and can easily be pushed into extreme poverty. Therefore, when education is being developed, it must be meaningful education that will compensate for any losses in the society and will lead to economic improvements. Such education programmes, therefore, have to provide, not just access to quality education. The programmes must meet the needs of the society and lead to cognitive development and the development of skills needed by that society to a level that will compensate for any short-term economic disadvantages. Education expansion that only focuses on access with simplistic quantitative measures will do more harm to the society than good. Education programmes that are developed with the partnership of those in the society, produce clear and beneficial learning outcomes which include both cognitive development and the acquisition of skills, intended to bring the society out of poverty, lead towards economic development, reduce its fragility and strengthen its quality of life.

For this to happen, donors and education planners may well need to revise their thinking and either greatly increase the resources available to education or accept that quality must be given precedence over quantity. This may mean a revision of the goal for universal long-term education for everyone in the immediate future, in order to achieve quality universal education in the longer term.

Questions for reflection

1. After reading this chapter, would you agree that spending on education should be increased, by both governments and aid agencies? What reservations would you put on such spending?

2. Education can impact positively on poverty alleviation and provide increased welfare even though actual earning powers of the people in question are not increased. In fact, such non-monetary benefits may be greater than any actual increase in earning capability. Could this be true? Can you give examples of how this could happen? Would it suggest a more or less egalitarian society?

3. Can you give examples from your own experience of either community-based education initiatives or formal education initiatives that have been successful? What has been the basis for their success?

Further reading

1. O'Grada, C. (2009) *Famine: A Short History*. New Jersey: Princeton University Press.

   Provides a refreshingly different perspective of famine, which reminds us that it is not a new phenomenon. The book explores a range of different causes and impacts of famines across the centuries, with good analysis of the interrelationships between famine, poverty and economic development.

2. Woessmann, H.L. (2008) The Role of Cognitive Skills in Economic Development 2008. *Journal of Economic Literature 46*(3), 607–668.

   The authors present a wide range of statistical evidence to support the thesis that the quality of education is crucial if there is to be an impact on economic development. It is a crucial article for anyone who wishes to speak with authority on this issue and one that depends heavily on statistical evidence.

3. Hawkes, D. and Ugur, M. (July 2012) *Evidence on the Relationship between Education, Skills and Economic Growth. – A Systematic Review*. London: EPPI-Centre, Institute of Education.

   Provides an overview of 39 different studies of the way education can impact economic development. The most useful outcome of this overview is a discussion of the lack of any agreement on what should be measured in terms of valid educational improvements.

4. Gove, A. and Wetterberg, A. (2011) *The Early Grade Reading Assessment*. North Carolina: RTI.

   Those who are interested in the actual learning outcomes in the first years of learning and how little many children are learning in school should read this very approachable book. It is an account of how Amber Gove and RTI have conducted reading assessments in a large number of developing countries.

References

Acana, S. (2006). *Reporting Results of National Assessment: Uganda Experience*, A paper presented at the 32nd Annual Conference of the Association for Educational Assessment, Singapore.

Africa Educational Trust. (2011). *Measuring Learning Achievements at Grade 4*. A paper presented to Education Development Committee for Somalia in 2012, Africa Educational Trust, Nairobi.

Asayo, O. (2011). The Abolition of Secondary School Fees in Kenya: Responses by the Poor*false. International Journal of Educational Development, 31*(4), 402–408.

Barro, R (1995). *Economic Growth*. New York: McGrath Hill, New York.

Brookings Institute. (2011). www.brookings.edu/research/reports/2011/06/09-global-impacts.

Chorlton, R. (2012). (UNICEF) Somalia Representative on the Release of a Rapid Assessment Study Presented to NGO's in Nairobi 2012, and Reported in Press Release August 2011, www.unicef.org/media_59492.html, Nairobi 2012.

Educational Statistical Abstracts. (2009). *Uganda Bureau of Statistics*. Kampala: Uganda Government.

Goldsmith, C. (2009). *Review of Current Status of Remuneration for Teachers and Other Education Employees*. Mimeograph (A Study for Somaliland and Puntland Ministries of Education) for AET and UNICEF. London.

Gove, A. and Wetterberg A. (2011). *The Early Grade Reading Assessment*. North Carolina: RTI.

Grada, C.O. (2009). *Famine: A Short History*. New Jersey: Princeton University Press.

Hanushek, E. and Woessmann, L. (2008). The Role of Cognitive Skills in Economic Development. *Journal of Economic Literature 46*(3), 607–668.

Hawkes, D. and Ugur, M. (2012). *Evidence on the Relationship between Education, Skills and Economic Growth. – A Systematic Review*. London University: EPPI-Centre, Institute of Education.

Hicks, R. (2002). *Impact Study of Non-Textbook Materials in Uganda Primary 1 & 2*. London: DFID.

—— (2006). *GWENU, Project Report*. London: DARET Impact Study Africa Educational Trust, mimeographed.

Hicks, C.C., McClanahan, T.R., Cinner, J.E. and Hills, J.M. (2009). Trade-offs in Values Assigned to Ecological Goods and Services Associated with Different Coral Reef Management Strategies. *Ecology and Society* 14, 10.

Hillman, A.L. and Jeneker, E. (2004). Educating Children in Poor Countries, *International Monetary Fund* http://www.imf.org/external/pubs/ft/issues/issues33/Washington.

Hussein, A. and Hicks, R. (Forthcoming). *Pastoralist Education and Training Programmes in Somalia and Somaliland, 2009–2011– An Impact Study*. London: Africa Educational Trust.

Jimenez, E. and Patrinos, H. (2008). *Human Development Network. Policy Research Working Paper 4568*. Washington DC: World Bank.

Kampala International University. (2012). Introduction to Computers, a first-year mimeographed module taken by all education students, also being taught in South Sudan. Kampala.

Kiros, G.E. and Hogan, D.B. (2001). War, Famine and Excess Child Mortality in Africa: The Role of Parental Education. *Journal of Epidemiology, 30*(3), 447–455.

Kratli, S (2001). Education Provision to Nomadic Pastoralists, *IDS Working Paper 126*, p. 7. London: IDS.

NESC. 2013, National Economic and Social Council of Kenya. *A Historical Perspective*, Government of Kenya, www.nesc.go.ke/index.

New Vision, November 10th 2012, Uganda www.newvison.co.ug/news/637176-upe-staggering-71-dropout.

Nkata, D. (2011). *Mid-Term Review of Strengthening Access and Participation in Secondary Education (SAPIS) Project*. London: Africa Educational Trust.

Nyerere, J. (1967). *Education for Self Reliance*, USA: University of Michigan.

O'Grada, C. (2009) *Famine: A Short History*. New Jersey: Princeton University Press.

Psacharoulos, G. (1985). Returns to Education: A Further International Update. *Journal of Human Resources, 20*(4), 583–604.

Raynor, J. (2009). *SOSSET End of Project Reports to EU Evaluating Their Funded Interventions in Puntland and Somaliland Secondary Education*. London: Africa Educational Trust.

Southern and Eastern Africa Consortium for Monitoring Education Quality (SACMEQ). (2013), Education Fact Sheet, Ministry of Education.

Thurow, R. (2012), Hay Festival *2013: Roger Thurow Looks at the Effects of Famine, The Telegraph*, 30th July 2013, London.

UNICEF. (2010) *Annual Report for Somalia*. Paris: UNICEF.

United Nations Conference on Trade and Development. (2001). *Economic Development in Africa 2*. pp. 4, 5, New York/Geneva.

UWEZO. (2012). *Are our Children Learning?* Nairobi: UWEZO East Africa.

Ward, M., Penny, A. and Read, T. (2006). *Education Reform in Uganda – 1997–2004. Reflections on Policy, Partenrship, Strategy and Implementation*, Researching Issues 60 London: DFID.

White House Press Release, Fact Sheet: Africa Education Initiative. (June 2002). Georgebush-whitehouse. archives.gov/news/releases/2002/06/20020620-18html (Fact sheet: Africa Education Initiative).

World Bank. (1990). *World Bank Development Report 1990*. New York: World Bank.

Understanding 'Education for All' in Contexts of Extreme Poverty: Experiences from Burkina Faso

2

Guillaume Charvon and Elaine Chase

Chapter Outline

Children who go to school don't know how to grow things anymore, and there aren't enough offices for everyone, so what are we going to do?

Introduction

As the Millennium Development Goals (United Nations 2000) approach the end of their term in 2015, a dialogue is underway to evaluate their achievements and consider what global targets for development might replace them (United Nations 2013). The second of these goals, universal primary *Education for All,* has posed particular challenges for countries with limited resources and where other complex social, cultural, economic and logistical constraints limit access to and participation in education. *Education for All* poses, therefore, complex questions about the meaning and value of education in societies facing extreme poverty and famine.

The United Nations human development index ranks Burkina Faso as 183 out of 187 countries globally, with 84 per cent of its population estimated as living in poverty according to the Multidimensional Poverty Index (UNDP 2013). Food scarcity and famine are major challenges, and in 2012 the country was ranked 46 out of 76 on the global hunger index (World Food Programme 2013). Famine is the result of a cumulation of natural disasters such as drought, floods and locusts which have led to increased desertification and reduced access to water and pasture land. Its land-locked position means that the country is also vulnerable to economic shocks such as sudden hikes in food prices which limit access to affordable food for the vast majority of people.

Within two or three generations, Burkinabe society has seen itself caught between two worlds: the world of *reproduction* – an agrarian/pastoral way of life; and the world of *innovation* – urban life, offering alternatives to the scarcity of arable land, and to which are attached certain ideas of social and economic success and well-being (such as access to electricity, running water, among others). The attractions of the latter have resulted in large demographic shifts and rapid social change accompanied by a growing tension between these two different ways of life.

Like other countries in sub-Saharan Francophone Africa, educational researchers in Burkina Faso have observed this tension reflected in the gap between the realities of family life and what children learn at school. One of the consequences of this disconnect is the perception that community life is not valued and that children who attend school seek ultimately to distance themselves from their family and their surroundings. Equally, parents may stop sending children to school, evidenced by the fact that the mean duration of school attendance for adults is just 1.3 years (UNDP 2013).

The generalized precariousness of life in terms of health, nutrition and access to water and education forces families to try and broker a balanced relationship between two modes of life with vastly different value systems: on the one hand a world structured by urbanization, increasing individualization and modernity; and on the other hand rural life, underpinned by notions of community and tradition. The contradiction between the school and the home environment outlined above is rooted in the difference between these different worlds and the sorts of knowledge required to exist and survive in each of them.

This chapter highlights the educational challenges for a society in transition from the often ignored or misunderstood perspectives of people living in extreme poverty. Allowing people to voice their own understandings of the difficulties they face offers new insights into the essence of the tension between the worlds of *reproduction* and *innovation* and the possibilities of achieving harmony between them. The chapter begins with a brief overview of the origins of action research and its methodology. It then goes on to present some of the key findings from the research before discussing their implications for the question of *Education for All* in Burkina Faso and beyond.

Methodology

In the social sciences, action research is characterized by its transformative impact on the reality of the subject of its investigation, and by the production of new knowledge about this reality (Freire 1972; 1974). The action research methodology employed in the current project was inspired by the transversal approach developed by Rene Barbier within his body of work on existential action research (1996). A fundamental principle underpins the method – the need to begin with people's own knowledge and expertise and not from an assumption of their ignorance. A wooden plaque displayed at the Burkina Faso headquarters in Ouagadougou captured this philosophy:

Let those who think they don't know anything teach those who think they do

The methodology works from the understanding that people with the most essential knowledge are those who struggle to make ends meet in the most difficult circumstances. It encompasses a radically different approach to orthodox social science in that it aims to produce knowledge with people rather than about them. Action research of this type incorporates two methodological components – *sharing knowledge* and *recognizing knowledge*. Combined, these lay the basis for *reconciling knowledge*, which, as we will see later, helps bridge the gap between the world of *reproduction* (tradition) and the world of *innovation* (modernity).

The action research project was carried out over a period of 18 months during 2011 and 2012, involving 335 men, women and children in urban and rural settings across Burkina Faso. The fundamental question underpinning the research was: *What knowledge do we need to build a future for everyone*? The topic relates directly to the meaning of *Education for All* in a country like Burkina Faso.

The work culminated in a seminar that took place during the first quarter of 2013 in Ouagadougou and involved 65 participants from Belgium, Central African Republic, Ethiopia, France, Great Britain, Mali, Senegal and from all the provinces of Burkina Faso. Participants were drawn from very different backgrounds and with different family, communal, professional or institutional responsibilities. While some had a university education, others had never picked up a pen; and while some had spent their lives working the land, others had never pulled a weed.

Findings from the wider research programme were incorporated into a process of knowledge sharing, which ensured that the ideas of those most likely to be excluded are placed at the heart of these interactions. The focus is on the reciprocal value of knowledge brought about through a permanent dialogue between community knowledge, expressed by those living in marginalized communities, and the knowledge of books and educational institutions. The transmission of knowledge is not structured on the idea of one-way exchange but on a dynamic of mutual and collective learning which assumes the fragmented nature of knowledge – no single person can know everything. Knowledge emerges as a collective construction carried out through three critical stages to which each person is able to make his or her contribution.

Time was first spent working and reflecting together in distinct groups made up of (a) representatives of national and international institutions, non-governmental organizations (NGOs) and universities; (b) those working in the field of education or related areas; and (c) families living in poverty and activists that work alongside them. This first stage is when each participant becomes conscious of the value of his or her life experience. Those living in extreme poverty and having been subjected to discrimination realize that everyone, not just those in poverty, shares the same goal of eradicating misery. Once this condition is in place, those in poverty can say things that would normally remain unspoken. As one young mother put it:

> Often, when I speak, I want to say certain things but the problem is that other thoughts come to me. Often when problems come into my head like that, I prefer not to say anything. I just let it go.[1]

The second critical stage consists of validating the legitimacy of each person's knowledge in peer groups. This enables each participant to move from the individual life experience towards constructing knowledge through dialogue with those people whose life experiences have forged similar understandings of the world to their own. The third stage is when the knowledge generated within the peer group is endorsed more widely and becomes recognized as established knowledge. This third stage is dialectic because it transmits the shared knowledge beyond the peer group to enrich other people's knowledge. From the point of view of action research, this wider exchange enables a growth in intelligence – that is, it enables participants to recognize how to expand the breadth of their understanding and ultimately to make valid judgements about the value of knowledge from other sources. Following are the themes that emerged from this work, both in terms of the process of research and its outcomes, which are relevant to the question of *Education for All*.

The relevance of action research to Education for All

The research revealed how those in poverty often feel that their own knowledge is dismissed as false, as one participant put it, '*people in poverty have no truth because even if what they say is true, others don't believe it*'. Thus action research, through creating an environment in which people are recognized for the first time as speaking the truth, promotes cohesion and inclusion of those most likely to be marginalized in society.

Throughout the action research, a degree of unity emerged between vastly different groups concerning the fundamental knowledge underpinning their lives, irrespective of whether it was acquired in academic circles, through school, the community or directly from experience. Several crossroads in the process illustrated how action research has the potential to identify common ground and mutual understanding between people with very different experiences; those in poverty discover the value of their knowledge and skills and others recognize its worth. In this way everyone begins to have a say and to play their part in the shared struggle for humanity. One participant in the research told the following fable that illustrates this point:

> One day in the bush, a chief invited all the animals to beat his millet. The elephant came and beat a lot of it. The buffalo managed to beat an impressive amount. Then the smallest of all frogs also joined in the work. Once all the work was done, the chief sent his supervisor to congratulate everyone. When he got to the two grains that the little frog had managed to beat, he became very angry and said, 'Is

UNIVERSITY OF WINCHESTER
LIBRARY

that all you can do, you lazy creature!' And he immediately dragged him before the chief. In front of the chief the frog explained himself, 'I didn't refuse to work but here's my stick and here is my hand. My hand did what it could with the stick that it had'. The chief, who was a just man, congratulated the frog, 'the little frog did not refuse to beat the millet, he took part in the shared task, let's not exclude him by humiliating him'. And everyone clapped.

Through giving equal value to different types of knowledge, this type of participatory action research encourages everyone to review the judgements they make about themselves and others; those having experienced the depths of poverty and exclusion suddenly find themselves recognized as experts in their own right. So, there is a shift from certain knowledge being unappreciated and associated with humiliation, towards knowledge which is recognized and accompanied by a sense of pride and inclusion. This was alluded to by one participant in the following way:

I have had many difficulties in my life. What I have lived through is not easy but it is nobody's fault. Today, if it wasn't for my children I could say that everything is fine. If it wasn't for my sister who lives on the streets in town and who I worry about, I could declare that my misery is over. When I say my misery is over, what does that mean? It's because people I didn't know before, and even those that I did, have become closer to me. That's why I can say that my misery is over. I am now among people.

Defining what constitutes knowledge

Throughout the research, participants identified at least four different types of accumulated knowledge, central to influencing them through life: knowledge that imbued them with a sense of resistance; knowledge that empowered them to hope for a better life; knowledge that bridged the realities of their traditional lives with the social and professional demands of the modern world; and an awareness that knowledge could be destructive, creating a rupture between the self and community.

Knowledge of resistance was said to derive from the harshness of life experiences and enabled people to face the daily demands of extreme poverty and its associated exclusion:

If you have suffered in life, you will know how to behave, but for someone who has never had to struggle, they would find it hard to deal with that life. Misery gives you advice... There are people who criticize me because I am poor, because I wear the same clothes every day.... They are right but the problem is that these people live their lives in a way that doesn't allow them to be my friends.

1. Knowledge of empowerment was largely associated with formal education and its promise of a 'better life', for children and grandchildren. Such knowledge was directed towards the future, even if it meant making sacrifices in the here and now as exemplified by the thoughts of these parents:

2. Whatever misery you face, don't allow your children to live it, do everything you can to send your children to school. Nowadays, I thank God, I sell second hand shoes to make-do but sometimes it is really difficult for me. If I manage to pay school fees this year, I pray that I don't have a problem next year.

In May, I take my children out of school to work in the fields. I do this because we have to have enough to eat and to be able to send the children to school the following year.

Knowledge bridging traditional and modern worlds was often described in terms of the skills acquired and transmitted through generations and which inscribe a process of intergenerational learning of fundamental knowledge:

My father sent me to live with my very old aunt who has never been to school. But she gave me knowledge about becoming a woman for the future. She worked in the fields and sold produce at the market. I learned from her how to grow things, how to sell the crops, she advised me. At the age of seven I was doing the same work as my aunt. She taught me good behaviour. From her I learned about respect for others. She taught me how to bring up children.

Likewise, knowledge gained from living in the family and community was also considered empowering because it lays the basis for learning in school. For example the respect taught within the family was seen as essential as the basis for learning in school.

Knowledge for a divided society

A strong theme that emerged throughout the research was the extent to which the educational choices for the majority of parents living in poverty are polarized around the possibilities of enabling their children to belong to one of two worlds outlined earlier on in the chapter: the world of *reproduction* – the agricultural and pastoral way of life, based on imitation and repetition; and the world of *innovation* – linked to the emergence of individual gains, rapid social transformation and technological change. The educational choices that parents make for their children are determined by their understandings and perceptions of these worlds and how they define the future.

Yet these choices are further complicated by the fact that the value sets which organize and orientate these worlds are often incompatible with each other. Even the modes of teaching they each use are contradictory. The world of *innovation* supposes the creativity of each generation, while that of *reproduction* rests on the repetition of methods, ideas and ways of doing things, from one generation to the next. As one woman put it:

> That [knowledge of reproduction] *is the knowledge of everyone, the knowledge my mother gave to me and that I have passed on to my daughter, you can't get better than that. What didn't my mother tell me: how to grow things and grind wheat, how to fetch water and firewood, how to go to the market – my mother taught me all of that. If you accept what she taught us, you will see that one day you can do anything.... I myself learned to prepare by watching others do it and when I tried to do it, I could. I watched carefully because I knew that it would do me good.*

School, the driver of the world of *innovation*, prioritizes the emergence of individuals while communitarian education, that of *reproduction*, situates the child in a social context where '*I*' never usurps the '*we*'. This subjection to the community, the driver of the world of *reproduction*, has less and less importance in the world of *innovation*. Hence success, whether shared or individual, only has meaning within specific contexts. What's more, the value systems on which these worlds are built are mutually exclusive and hence incompatible, explaining the disconnection suggested in the introduction to this chapter. Useful knowledge in one world is determined as useless in the other. If a child learns to grow crops, this knowledge has limited relevance if he or she identifies with an idea of success linked to city life. And conversely, theoretical knowledge gained in school may have no direct relevance to the realities of village life:

> They say that if you don't go to school you won't have knowledge ... but we know that there are those who did go to school and who don't have the knowledge that others have; and others who have not gone to school and who have knowledge.

Participants repeatedly reflected on how different understandings of knowledge influence wider processes of inclusion and exclusion. For example, school is uniformly presented as a tool for empowerment. Research in recent years in Burkina Faso (ATD Fourth World 2004) has, however, shown how children who attended primary school but have been unable, usually due to family difficulties or lack of resources, to proceed to secondary school often end up living on the street; they fit neither in the world of *reproduction* nor in the world of *innovation*. Conversely, children who have rarely or never been to school often reconnect more easily with their families.

The meaning of educational success

Participants' views about what signified educational success were inevitably tied to their own understandings of what constituted the most valid and useful knowledge for their daily lives. Nonetheless, the action research and the seminar generated some consensus concerning basic values which were vital for everyone to succeed in educational terms.

Solidarity and mutual support were seen as a fundamental pre-requisite for learning, especially in circumstances of extreme poverty. One man who earned his living through begging on the streets spoke of how when one of his children's friends came from school not having eaten, he took 100 CFA francs (0.15 euro) from his box and gave it to him, even though he did not know if he would have anything to give his own children that day. Another example was given of a child who had to repeat the first year of school five years in a row because his mother could not afford to pay the annual supplement of 1,500 CFA francs (2.29 euros). The child started to become violent and alienated himself from others. The teacher offered to pay some of the contribution and the child was appointed as class prefect. Gradually he regained trust and confidence and was able to succeed.

Educational success was also thought to be reflected in values of respect, forgiveness, humility, courage and dignity not only for oneself but also for others. One girl said,

> When my friends went off somewhere to eat and I had no money, I preferred to say that I wasn't hungry, rather than admit that my father had nothing to give me. That would show a lack of respect for him. I passed the BEPC [exam] with an empty stomach, but I didn't tell my friends that my father hadn't given me anything to eat, I said that I was too preoccupied by the exam to eat.

Success was also defined in terms of becoming useful to self, family, community and society as a whole. Those who became a reference point in their communities, who guided others and were consulted for advice, typified what it meant to be successful. This notion of educational success as being useful to oneself and others implies a sense of belonging to a community – being able to acquire knowledge, share it with others and then collectively put it into practice. As one participant put it:

> Knowledge that is most important to me is being able to get people together so that those who know things teach those who don't, so that collectively we can exploit this knowledge. Nowadays we don't listen to those who are in poverty but we do listen to those who are better off. Yet those who don't have anything may sometimes have really good ideas for us. We have to do everything we can to listen to them.

Many participants defined the essence of knowledge not as the means for becoming 'master and possessor of nature' (Descartes 1637) but as the basis for belonging to a community of other humans. Knowledge makes sense when it creates cohesion within a community around a set of shared values. These values have to be learned and they constitute a body of knowledge in their own right, sustaining social ties and enabling people to live together in ways shaped by culture. From the perspective of those living in extreme poverty, this knowledge is fundamental because the security of existence and the ability to feel human amongst humans depends on it. This vision of educational success thus emerges as a project understood as discovering knowledge that unites society as a whole.

Factors that prevent educational success

However, the achievement of this shared vision for educational success, grounded in the experience of community, was thought to be constantly challenged by the evolution of modern society, by the daily constraints imposed by extreme poverty and, as noted earlier, by a growing division within society into two separate worlds.

The research and the seminar during which the findings were discussed revealed several fundamental factors that got in the way of attaining educational success. An absence of birth certificates for many children was a recurrent concern, one mother describing the certificate as '*the first diploma of life*' without which children could not be enrolled in schools. Others described long periods of sickness during which children could not attend school either because they were ill themselves or because they were caring for others who were ill.

Overcrowded classes and de-motivated teachers, the irrelevance of the school curricula and the hidden costs of education, such as the contributions for school meals or to the parent teachers associations, all created further barriers to accessing school for many. Yet there were also other social challenges described, such as discrimination, humiliation, mockery and violence, typically experienced by those in poverty (see Walker et al. 2013). One parent explained,

> *One day my daughter said to me, 'Papa, they told me at the school that it is pointless me studying and that I will never have my certificate because my father is poor. He empties the public toilets, he makes ropes in order to sell them.*

And one young man describing his earlier experience of school said,

> *When I was in class it was hard. The teacher said to me, 'your mother can't buy you a school bag!' And they made fun of me. Some pupils were laughing. As I was only a child, I was ashamed and I often got angry. That's how violence begins.*

Hunger and famine emerged as further challenges to learning for many children and their families. People spoke of how the climatic conditions of Burkina Faso often affected food production and generated sometimes extended periods of famine across the country. Hunger was said to affect the lives of communities living in poverty in a number of ways. At a very basic level, it made learning extremely difficult:

> *You get up, you have eaten nothing, you leave for school with a cramping stomach. Who is going to get up in the morning have a small bowl of millet and go to school? On top of eating the small bowl of millet, I think it is the efforts of our parents that are in our hearts. Our parent's efforts are like a meal, it was that which filled our stomachs so that we could carry on.*
>
> *When my daughter went to school, our main worry was hunger, because it was hunger that was killing us. So we would send our child to school but a child can't learn if they are hungry.*

Secondly, hunger was also considered to be central to the relationships between families living in extreme poverty and the communities they belong to. Hunger, it was said, generated such a powerful obstacle to educational success that it was possible to succeed only if families and communities pulled together. In reality, however, families were increasingly forced to choose between preserving their dignity and subjecting themselves to humiliation in order to survive. As one participant put it,

> *Sometimes they give us leftovers on dirty plates. It makes us feel bad, but what can we do?*

More broadly, hunger was described as threatening the social bonds within communities. Families in extreme poverty were constantly posed with the dilemma of how to belong to a community when they had nothing to share. This concern was coupled with a profound sense that any collective responsibility for each other within communities was diminishing in modern society, as one participant put it;

> Today, man has less pity in his heart. He only looks after his brother, his child and his wife. But if you are poor, you don't have a wife or a brother... who is going to look after you? And who are you going to look after?

The meaning of Education for All

The wider question concerning what *Education for All* means in a country like Burkina Faso is illustrated by the following quote from one participant in the research:

> If educational success is to work in offices or be a politician, I can say that amongst the poor, those who succeed are very few. That is why so many families living in poverty stop sending their children to school. That is why I suggest that at school they also teach children training in how to do things. If they did that, then we could believe that school is for everyone.

In effect, parents are often forced to take a gamble over which world their children should stake a claim to, a gamble which has several consequences. First, it results in parents choosing to assign their children to different worlds. Within the same family, some will go to school while others will stay and learn about agricultural and pastoral life. Since success is understood collectively rather than on an individual basis, the chances of success for the whole family are thus increased through the diversity of the choices made.

The demands for children to fit into either one world or the other generate a major stumbling block for policies concerning *Education for All*. It's not a lack of understanding on the part of the school about how to enlighten parents which undermines such policies, but rather their rational underlying value system. At the heart of the world of *reproduction*, socio-economic success is concentrated within the family to enable them to face the precariousness of the family's existence. Does it make sense, therefore, to choose a single pathway towards success for all while the future of the whole community depends on it? After all, the pathway that takes children through school and leads to regular paid activity in town is just as precarious and is no more likely to offer security. Taken within this reference system, choices made by parents are logical and rational, emanating from the sense of collective determinism at work within the world of *reproduction*. Hence as one parent put it, *'of my nine children, two are going to school, the girls are going to learn about work within the family, the others will look after the cattle in the fields'*.

Yet, from the point of view of the world of *innovation* to which are attached values of empowerment and freedom, such choices are not morally acceptable; why should some have the chance to go to school and not others? Each logic drawing its reference from its own value system, and these systems being exclusive of each other, there is no real meeting point through which one world can influence the other. And value systems that do not meet tend to become value systems which are judgemental of each other:

> At school, one learns to become a big person. A big person is what? It is someone that works in an air-conditioned office. At home, one learns what you need to be able help the family survive tomorrow, when your parents aren't there any longer.

What emerges therefore is an inherent uselessness of knowledge produced in one world when it is transferred to the other – '*Children who go to school, no longer want to grow crops*'. Here we stress that it is not a lack of knowledge that creates an incapacity to use your abilities for the good of society, but the irrelevance of such knowledge to the world in which it is to be applied. In other words, each world sees the knowledge of the other as useless because they each employ their own value systems and attach very different values to different types of knowledge.

From the point of view of putting in place policies for *Education for All* – predominantly a view of *education* relevant to the world of *innovation* – it is imperative to address the fundamental chasm between these radically different value systems. In order to be effective, those implementing these policies must begin to appreciate the knowledge base within the world of *reproduction* and how easy it is to misconstrue it as irrelevant when one belongs to the world of *innovation*. Given the dominance and power inherent in the world of *innovation*, it is only through actively engaging people living in extreme poverty in dialogue that we can begin to break down these silos and really understand what *Education for All* means for the whole of society.

Participants in the research were acutely aware of the tensions between these two worlds. They expressed concern that the modern education system in Burkina Faso often represents the antithesis of the sorts of traditional education they value and undermines the importance of hard physical work. They spoke of the enormous efforts to educate their children which remained largely unrecognized by the formal education system. As one participant put it:

> *Traditional knowledge and specialized knowledge should complement each other. Unfortunately, however, there is a tension between them. Those who have been to school take one side and think they are always right. And those who haven't been to school take their side and believe that the others have made a mistake and are wrong. But I think this is unfortunate because we have to pull all this knowledge together. If not, then those who have learned traditional ways and those who learned from school can never be reunited.*

Importantly, however, participants also gave examples of their efforts to reconcile different types of knowledge and to keep their children grounded in both worlds:

> *I have chosen to send my children to school but it is not school alone that will enable them to succeed. I send my sons to sell things during the holidays. That experience will also give them opportunities; that way they understand that it is not only school that gives success. Even if they don't succeed at school they will have other ways of making ends meet.*
>
> *What our parents bequeathed to us as knowledge and what we learned at the school, I can say often do not go hand in hand – but it often requires work to reconcile these two forms of knowledge so that in the end there is no contradiction. Because what I learn at school, I can say is beneficial for me, the knowledge I gained from my parents I consider as traditional, also beneficial for me. I always think about how best to combine these types of knowledge and move forward.*

Discussion and conclusion

The process of action research and the seminar which drew it all together developed a shared vision of the meaning *of Education for All*, what prevents it and what might enable it to be attained. The question of what is knowledge – its acquisition and transmission, its underlying values and its usefulness – brings out the tensions within Burkinabe society as it struggles for harmony between community and global value systems and considers the meaning of *Education for All*. This observation is not new; the tension between local and global knowledge has been examined in previous research and certain key lessons have been drawn (Tourneaux 2011). Such work has shown, for example, that the exclusive use of French penalizes those children whose parents cannot speak it. Equally that developing appropriate educational curricula is not just a question of taking educational programmes conceptualized in French or English and translating them into African languages, but ensuring that languages and local knowledge are integrated into the educational system so that it is possible to bring about endogenous social change. Nonetheless, significant challenges remain which typify the difficulties faced by Burkina Faso in implementing the Millennium Development Goal of *Education for All*. The persistence of these challenges makes it imperative to continue to pay attention to them.

One way of approaching and beginning to understand this tension with respect to education is to consider the social representations at work – the ways in which society communicates and teaches about the social, material and ideological environment (Jodelet 1984). Our analysis shows that the possible tensions relating to different understandings of knowledge and educational success arise out of an incompatibility between systems which renders them entirely exclusive of each other. In addition, such analysis allows us to specify the nature of this incompatibility in relation to education and to think about its consequences.

In our view, the failure to effectively implement policies offering *Education for All* is linked to a presupposition, itself dependent exclusively on the social representations contained in the world of *innovation*, of society's responsibility to eradicate ignorance. The reality is, however, that such policies are not responding to ignorance but to knowledge. Yet, since the exclusivity of these worlds means that where one has knowledge in one world it is not recognized as valid in the other, these different types of knowledge remain unappreciated, unless there is commitment to reconcile them.

The participatory research reported on here demonstrates one approach towards achieving a degree of reconciliation between these different worlds. We have seen that the original principle which underpins and gives meaning to basic knowledge is the capacity of such knowledge to nurture a sense of belonging. In a cultural context where the community is paramount and gives meaning to the individual, it is these social ties which support the transmission of knowledge. Speaking of our cultural activities in rural and urban environments, many parents told us, '*it is good what you are doing, you reunite children and with that they learn*'.

Educational for All appears to depend on several things. Bringing about educational policies rooted in shared knowledge and understanding necessitates a permanent dialogue between the family, the community and the school. This must ensure the involvement of everyone and should recognize that each child belongs to a diversified and expansive educational community encompassing different conceptualizations of educational success. The methodology presented in this chapter allows the generation of shared knowledge grounded in the lived experience and values of those living in extreme poverty. The process of reconciling different types of knowledge helps bridge the gap between the world of *reproduction* (that of tradition) and the world of *innovation* (that of modernity).

To put in place educational policies which are for everyone and adapted to their environments, it is necessary to start from appreciating the knowledge base of any community and not from the presumption of ignorance. Facilitating the sharing and uniting of different types of knowledge provides the basis for designing an educational system that is really for everyone. The ways in which we have worked through these pilot projects to ensure dialogue between the environment and school in order to generate a common educational project could be replicated in other contexts.

From the perspective of international institutions that make their case on the evidence available, it should be remembered that those in extreme poverty have high expectations of school because it offers the promise of social inclusion compared to a community which often alienates and excludes them. As one mother put it, '*I send my children to school because I don't want them to lead the same life that I have known*'. If we are to respond to the expectations of populations who have been repeatedly socially excluded, schools with the mission of *Education for All* must support and strengthen learning about the dynamics of belonging and in this way satisfy the ambition of this mother.

The need for dialogue between the different actors within the educational community has to be integrated into global policies on *Education for All*, paying particular attention to strengthening cooperation between all its actors – between children, between teachers and pupils and between teachers and families. Building such cooperation requires each actor to recognize the contribution of the others within the educational community and to understand how these different contributions complement each other.

For researchers and universities, we learn that the concept of education has to be expanded to include work on understanding conceptualizations of basic knowledge and what constitutes educational success; being useful to oneself, to the family and having a sense of belonging to the community and to society. Researchers from the universities who participated in this process of understanding knowledge also questioned their own responsibilities concerning this quest for *Education for All*. As one explained,

> We often think that if we listen carefully to what people tell us about their daily struggles, we can analyse their words and come up with some good solutions to present to those who have positions of responsibility: the government, policy makers, representatives of international organizations etc. But, the problem with this approach is that something is missing, we lose the opportunity to enable people to find their own solutions to these problems and so our research methods are inherently limited. A major challenge for us is to think about how we can work better with people living in extreme poverty across the world so that they discover and voice their own solutions.

For those who have faced the daily struggles of resisting extreme poverty, the experience of action research was enlightening, summarized here:

> We knew that we had ideas and that these ideas are important for others. We have understood that understanding life enables us to change it. These words that have been said, they remind us of what we know, but we have forgotten and now we can apply this knowledge and the whole country can move forward.

Education clearly has the potential for alleviating extreme poverty in countries such as Burkina Faso in economic, social and political terms. Provided there is a supportive economic environment, it may widen opportunities and choices and increase financial capacity, thus improving the quality of people's lives. Equally, it can play a significant role in reducing social marginalization, giving people greater control over their lives and sustaining systems of good governance. As we have seen in this chapter, however, the capacity of education to enhance economic, social and human capital is contingent on education systems being relevant and appropriate to the context in which they are designed and implemented. Understanding where formal educational provision sits within the wider context of children and young people's lives; recognizing the importance of the learning that takes place outside of as well as within the school context; and being cognizant of the cultural norms, values and expectations of parents and the wider community are all vital in creating educational provisions which support economic, social and human development. As we have outlined here, such understanding comes from a continuous process of dialogue, interaction and mutual learning between educational structures and the wider communities they are intended to serve.

> ## Questions for reflection
>
> 1. What are the implications of this work in Burkina Faso for the attainment of *Education for All* at a global level?
> 2. What relevance does 'modern' education have for people living in situations of extreme poverty across the world?
> 3. What sorts of educational interventions are most likely to reconcile traditional rural life with the demands of modern life?

Acknowledgements

The findings presented in this chapter are from a project conducted by the ATD (Agir Tous pour La Dignity – All Together in Dignity) Fourth World movement, which has worked in Burkina Faso for almost 30 years, striving to promote solidarity among those facing extreme poverty and exclusion. http://www.atd-fourthworld.org/International-Movement-ATD-Fourth.html (Accessed 15 July 2013). Our sincere thanks go to all those who took part in the action research project and who shared their experiences.

Notes

1 The quotes used throughout the chapter are anonymized extracts taken from the action research which were filmed and used (with participants' permission) as prompts for discussion throughout the seminar in Ouagadougou.

Further reading

1. Freire, P. (1972) *Pedagogy of the Oppressed*. London: Penguin

The work of Paulo Freire has been vital in critically analysing how we conceptualize education and learning as a process of empowerment. Freire's notion of conscientization emphasizes the process of developing critical awareness of social reality through collective reflection and action.

2. Fourth World University Research Group, (2007) *The Merging of Knowledge: People in Poverty and Academics Thinking Together*. University Press of America

This text offers practical insights into how academics have worked in close partnership with people living in poverty to design and carry out research to inform poverty alleviation strategies.

3. Godinot, X. (Ed.) (2012) *Eradicating Extreme Poverty: Democracy, Globalisation and Human Rights*. London: Pluto Press

This text argues for a development approach to alleviate poverty which enables people experiencing it to have a voice in formulating solutions grounded in the realities of their lives. It encourages an understanding of poverty that looks beyond material deprivation to the psychological and social impact of poverty and how best to promote people's dignity.

References

ATD Fourth World (2004). *How Poverty Separates Parents and Children: A Challenge to Human Rights*. Méry-Sur-Oise: Fourth World Publications.

—— (2012). *Guidelines for the Merging of Knowledge and Practices When Working with People Living in Situations of Poverty and Social Exclusion*. Available at: http://www.atd-fourthworld.org/ Guidelines-for-the-Merging-of.html (accessed 18 June 2013).

Barbier R. (1996). La Recherche Action. Paris, Economica, col. Anthropos.

Descartes, R. (1637). *Discourse on Method*. Vol. XXXIV, Part 1. The Harvard Classics. New York: P.F. Collier & Son, 1909–1914.

Freire, P. (1972). *Pedagogy of the Oppressed*. London: Penguin.

Freire, P. (1974). *Education for Critical Consciousness*. London: Continuum.

Jodelet, D. (1984). Représentations sociales: phénomènes, concepts et théorie. In: S. Moscovici, *Psychologie sociale*. Paris: PUF, pp. 357–378. (Trans: Social Representations: phenomena, concepts and theory In S. Moscovici, *Social Psychology*).

Tourneux, H. (2011). *La transmission des savoirs en Afrique. Savoirs locaux et langues locales pour l'enseignement*, Paris: Karthala (Trans: The transmission of knowledge in Africa. Teaching with local knowledge and local languages).

UNDP (2013). *Human Development Report, Burkina Faso*. Available at: http://hdrstats.undp.org/en/ countries/profiles/bfa.html (accessed 19 June 2013).

United Nations (2000). *Millennium Development Goals*. Available at: http://www.un.org/ millenniumgoals/ (accessed 18 June 2013).

United Nations (2013). *We Can End Poverty 2015 Millennium Development Goals*. Available at: http:// www.un.org/millenniumgoals/beyond2015-news.shtml (accessed 15 July 2013).

Walker, R., Bantebya Kyomuhendo, G., Chase, E., Chouudhry, S., Gurbrium, E.LØdemel, I, Mathew, L., Mwiine, A., Pellissery, S and Yan, M (2013). Poverty in Global Perspective: Is shame a common denominator. *Journal of Social Policy*, 42, 2, 215–233.

World Food Programme (2013). *Burkina Faso Overview*. Available at: http://www.wfp.org/countries/ burkina-faso/overview (accessed 18 June 2013).

Access to Education, Poverty, Malnutrition and Health in Bangladesh

Benjamin Zeitlyn and Altaf Hossain

3

Chapter Outline

Introduction

This chapter explores the strong relationships between exclusion from education, poverty, malnutrition and poor health in Bangladesh, drawing on the empirical and conceptual work of the Consortium for Research on Educational Access, Transitions and Equity (CREATE). Using CREATE's conceptual model of 'zones of exclusion' and the detailed data collected in Bangladesh as part of the consortium's work, the chapter describes the relationships between exclusion from education, poverty, malnutrition and health. The chapter argues that these complex and multidirectional relationships point to a need to tackle problems of exclusion from education, nutrition and health together.

Pridmore's (2007) review of research evidence summarizes the multiple links between nutrition and access to education. A range of common and interlinked health and nutritional problems cause cognitive damage, reduce motivation and the capacity for concentration and therefore affect the capacity of children for learning. As a result, they are more likely to repeat grades, progress slowly through the grades, drop out of school and perform poorly in school (Pridmore 2007, p. 33). Diseases such as malaria and parasitic worms lead to reduced cognition and stunting, and are reasons for late enrolment in school (Pridmore 2007, p. 19). Children who enrol late in school are often out of school until the age of 8 or 10 and then become over-age for their grade and tend to drop out earlier, attend infrequently and have poor learning outcomes. In Bangladesh, where childhood malnutrition is endemic, these relationships have emerged from research (Ahmed, et al. 2005; Tarleton et al. 2006; Grira 2004).

Once in school, children who suffer or have suffered from malnutrition continue to be disadvantaged. Tarleton's et al. (2006) research shows that stunting and low height-for-age and weight-for-age at age of enrolment was associated with low scores at cognitive tests of school-age children. Many irreversible health problems are caused by poor nutrition and health in pregnancy and early childhood, well before the age of enrolment. Helmers and Patnam's (2010) work on Andhra Pradesh in India suggests that indicators of health in very young children have a significant bearing on subsequent cognitive and non-cognitive skill acquisition.

The importance of poor health, nutrition and disability as factors associated with exclusion from education suggests the need for policy initiatives that address nutrition, health, disability and education concerns together. In particular, this chapter suggests that vaccination programmes, and other forms of child health programmes, could reduce the numbers of children who enrol late or never enrol, as well as improving the attendance and performance of children who are in school. Few of the schools surveyed had facilities to treat sick children, teachers trained to identify health problems, or student health records.

Access to education is often measured by enrolment. Net enrolment ratios and primary completion rates are used to measure progress towards Education for All and Millennium Development Goals (MDGs), specifically MDG 2 – to achieve universal primary education by 2015. However, Lewin (2007) examines and expands the notion of access, arguing that enrolment is only part of the process and describing the real desirable outcome as 'meaningful access'. According to Lewin, access to education is not meaningful unless it results in:

1. Secure enrolment and regular attendance;
2. Progression through grades at appropriate ages;
3. Meaningful learning which has utility;
4. Reasonable chances of transition to lower secondary grades, especially where these are within the basic education cycle.
5. More rather than less equitable opportunities to learn for children from poorer households, especially girls, with less variation in quality between schools (Lewin 2007, p. 21).

This definition of meaningful access is the basis of CREATE's broad view of access and conceptual model. To measure access to education, this chapter uses indicators of access to education that relate to the 'zones of exclusion' outlined by Lewin (2007): access to pre-school (zone 0), levels of children never enrolled (zone 1), children who drop out of school (zones 2 and 5) and children who are at risk of exclusion or 'silently excluded' (zones 3 and 6). This model helps us to understand access to and exclusion from education in more depth, disaggregating 'out of school children' into groups depending on the nature of their exclusion. This, in turn, helps to develop appropriate policy recommendations for different types of exclusion. It is clear, for example, that the problems which mean that some children have never been to school at all are not the same as those which lead to many children dropping out of school. In many contexts, there are many more children who have dropped out of school among 'out of school children' than those who have never enrolled. These insights can lead to important policy decisions.

The identification of silently excluded children is, by its very nature, difficult. To identify these children, household and school surveys, conducted in two rounds in 2007 and 2009, used three indicators of silent exclusion identified by Lewin (2007):

- Low attendance: the child is aged 6–15 and the parent reported that the child was absent from school for more than one day in the past week.
- Low achievement: the child is aged 6–15 and their parent ranked child as being in the 'bottom 25 per cent' of the class.
- Repetition: the child is aged 6–15 and their parents report that the child has repeated a year of school at least once.

This chapter focuses on zones 1, 2 and 3, which refer to children excluded from basic education, either because they have never entered school, they have dropped out of school or they are nominally enrolled but are attending infrequently, performing poorly or repeating years. The chapter uses these definitions of educational exclusion, and data from the 2007 and 2009 rounds of the 'Community and School Survey' (ComSS) in Bangladesh. The ComSS was based in six locations, one in each administrative division of Bangladesh, and included 6,696 households and 36 schools, and a total of 9,045 children aged between 4 and 15. It is an exclusively rural survey with a pro-poor bias.

Education in Bangladesh

The recent history of education in Bangladesh is generally one of increases in levels of enrolment and levels of gender equality. Between 1980 and 2004, enrolment in primary education increased from 8 million to 18 million children (Ahmed et al. 2007, p. 4). Bangladesh has achieved gender parity in enrolment at both primary and secondary education levels (World Bank, 2008; Raynor and Wesson 2006, p. 3). There has been significant progress and these are great achievements for Bangladesh. However, as discussed above, enrolment is only part of the story and does not guarantee meaningful access. Despite increases in enrolment, girls in Bangladesh are still less likely to complete secondary school, gain an academic qualification, study subjects that have a good marketable value, or to move on to paid employment. Girls are still significantly less likely to be entered for secondary school exams or to pass them – so despite equal enrolment what happens in school and after school is not equal (Raynor and Wesson 2006, p. 7). In this way gender equality in enrolment in education in Bangladesh illustrates the concept of meaningful access.

Public spending on education has ranged between 2.2 and 2.5 per cent of GDP over the last decade – meaning that Bangladesh spends less on education than many of its neighbours and comparable countries. Bangladesh has a short, five-year cycle of primary school and survival rates to the last grade of primary school did not show sustained improvements between 1994 and 2004 and remained about 55 per cent throughout the period (Ahmed et al. 2007, p. 16). In 2008, the survival rate to the last grade of primary school was 52 per cent (Ahmed, M. 2011, p. 9). In terms of learning outcomes, there has been modest progress in recent years, but tests of 'basic competencies' (designed for all primary school leavers to be able to complete) show that on average, a third are not achieved by grade five graduates (Ahmed, M. 2011, p. 8). Clearly, there remain problems and challenges ahead for Bangladesh to achieve meaningful access to education for all, higher levels of quality and better outcomes from education.

Factors associated with exclusion from and poor achievement in primary education in Bangladesh identified and analysed in the literature include low income (Grira 2004), low levels of parental education (Ahmed, S. 2011; Khanam et al. 2011; Grira 2004), child labour (Ahmed, S. 2011; Arends-Kuenning and Amin 2004), gender (Arends-Kuenning and Amin 2004; Raynor and Wesson 2006; Asadullah and Chaudhury 2009), corruption (Choe et al. 2013), health (Driessen et al. 2011, Grira 2004), malnutrition (Grira 2004), proximity to a primary school (Grira 2004) or secondary school (Khanam et. al. 2011), being from a household where the head is non-Muslim (Grira 2004), sibling order (Grira 2004) and school type (Hossain and Zeitlyn 2010).

In reality, many of these factors are linked, combine with one another or are interrelated to such a degree that analysis of one without controls for the others risks problems of endogeneity, as Grira (2004) points out in a study of determinants of grade attainment in Bangladesh. Almost all education research done in Bangladesh has identified strong correlations between various indicators of poverty and exclusion from education at all levels of the education system (Al-Samarrai 2009; Khanam et al. 2011; Grira 2004). Some of the factors described above are related to poverty directly and obviously as causes and effects of poverty are widely used as indicators of poverty. These include low income, low levels of parental education, child labour, poor health and malnutrition. These are all direct causes and/or consequences of poverty.

Some of the factors have more tangential and perhaps cultural or political relationships to poverty. These might include corruption, which as Choe et al. (2013) find, is more likely to affect poor families. Proximity to a non-government or community primary school rather than a better funded government primary school is strongly associated with poverty (Hossain and Zeitlyn 2010). Relationships between gender, poverty and educational attainment run in both directions depending on the level of education and the context, with girls sometimes being said to be less well represented at primary level than boys for 'religious' reasons (Ahmed 2011) and boys sometimes being less well represented at secondary level than girls due to the incentives created by the girl's secondary stipend programme and higher opportunity costs for boys (Arends-Kuenning and Amin 2004). Social exclusion and persecution of religious and ethnic minorities in Bangladesh leads both to their relative poverty and to their exclusion from education (Grira 2004). All of the factors related to exclusion can be related to poverty in some way. In this chapter, we focus mainly on the interlinked relationships between health, poverty and exclusion from education.

Grira (2004) and Knanam et al. (2011) strangely conflate child health with nutritional status, rather than seeing the two as distinct but related. They use indicators of malnutrition as proxies for child health, rather than looking at the very significant effects of sickness which may lead to the strange finding that child 'health', measured as long-term malnutrition, was not significantly related to current attendance (Khanam et al. 2011, p. 449). The findings of Grira's (2004) paper, that low weight for age (a general indicator of malnutrition) does not have a significant impact on enrolment but does have a significant impact on on-time progression through the grades, are surprising given that there is strong evidence that over-age children are more likely to drop out of school and that dropout is closely correlated to age (Hossain, A. 2010; Hunt 2008, p. 13; Lewin 2007, p. 25; Khanam et al. 2011). Khanam et al. (2011) find that not only is age a strong determinant of grade attainment (due to the increasing opportunity costs of education as a child gets older), but that stunting (low height for age) is significantly related to both enrolment and grade attainment.

The ComSS database contains data on health *and* nutritional status so these can be analysed separately as well as together. This chapter mainly draws on indicators of health, relating to sickness, immunization, visits from health workers and a basic indicator of malnutrition (height) and relates these to poverty (measured by income and food security) and access to education. Self-reported poor health (the indicator used in this chapter) is significantly correlated with other indicators of poverty. Perhaps surprisingly, low weight and low height are weakly, and mostly insignificantly, correlated with other indicators of poverty apart from each other. They are, however, both significantly correlated with self-reported poor health.

This indicates that children from households with relatively high income are equally likely to be low weight and low height as those from relatively low-income households and that these indicators of poverty capture different children from the others. Deolalikar (2005) reports very high levels of child malnutrition among the poorest in Bangladesh using Demographic and Health Survey (DHS) data. In the lowest quintile, more than 60 per cent of children aged between 6 and 71 months were stunted, while more than

25 per cent were severely stunted. However, about a third of the richest quintile of children in the country, who do not have problems of affording food, were also malnourished. This indicates that beyond consumption measures of poverty there are cultural and social issues that are important in determining child malnutrition in Bangladesh (Deolalikar 2005, p. 63). Despite these intriguing findings, poverty remains importantly associated with nutritional status, health status and educational exclusion.

Primary education is free and compulsory in Bangladesh; textbooks are also provided free. However, there remain other direct and opportunity costs of education, which prevent the poorest from participating. The government and development partners have designed various ways of tackling these problems. Building upon the success of the Food for Education programme in the 1990s, the government of Bangladesh has set up stipend schemes to pay for some of these costs for the poor and for girls. However, most of the available evidence suggests that the stipend schemes have not effectively targeted the poorest, who are still significantly excluded from basic education, in terms of never-enrolment, dropout and silent exclusion (Tietjen 2003; Baulch 2010; Al-Samarrai 2009; Hossain and Zeitlyn 2010; Hossain N. 2010).

Poverty and educational access in Bangladesh

Poverty is complex and multidimensional, and can be measured in different ways. This chapter uses two relatively simple measures of poverty, one is monthly household income and the other is food security. Food security status can be used as proxy for overall economic status. Respondents in the ComSS were asked to recall and make an assessment of income and expenditure of all the members of the household during the previous year, with help from the interviewer. They were then asked to place themselves in one of the four categories in regard to perceived food security in the household – always in deficit, sometimes in deficit, sufficient to meet the needs, and surplus.

ComSS data showed that 12 per cent of the total households suffered from constant food insecurity, while around one third of the households suffered from intermittent food insecurity. A little over a third had enough to meet their food security needs, whereas only 18.8 per cent were in the surplus food security category. These groups correlated with poverty by income (Table 3.1).

Table 3.1 Food security and income

	Mean monthly household income in Bangladeshi Taka	Mean monthly household income in US dollars	Number of households
Always in deficit	3,074.22	44.55	772
Sometimes in deficit	4,353.39	63.09	2,022
Have enough/break even	5,824.43	84.41	2,452
Surplus	10,809.55	156.66	1,204
Average/Total	5,964.66	86.44	6,450

Source: ComSS 2009.

Ninety per cent of individuals in this sample lived below the US $1 per day poverty line and 75 per cent lived below the US ¢50 per day poverty line. So, within this very poor sample, the relationships between poverty and indicators of access to education assess the very poor relative to the poor. We use a composite measure of educational exclusion, which incorporates all three zones of exclusion, and investigate the relationships between this and indicators of poverty in terms of income, food insecurity and health. The very large proportion of the sample who are income poor means that there is a weak and insignificant relationship between being income poor and excluded from education using this composite measure. More detailed examinations of the relationships between income poverty and the different zones of educational exclusion suggest that this is still an important indicator, as we shall see. However, the indicators relating to food security status and health emerge as being more strongly and significantly correlated with educational exclusion. Poor health is also significantly associated with low income and food insecurity, suggesting that targeting poor people who suffer from health problems for interventions designed to improve access to and continuation in education could be an effective way of improving access to education.

Evidence from many studies shows that educational access is strongly determined by household income (Lewin 2007; Filmer and Pritchett 2001). Although primary education is free and compulsory in Bangladesh, research indicates that there are substantial additional private costs and opportunity costs of education that parents must meet for their children's schooling (Ahmad, et al. 2007, Ahmed et al. 2005). These costs include examination fees, private tuition and paying for notebooks in the upper grades of primary school.

The household survey indicates that the average cost per child per year of attending primary school was Tk. 3,812 (about US $55), slightly more for boys (Tk. 3,935) and slightly less for girls (Tk. 3,692). The average yearly income per person was Tk. 14,315.18 or around US $207 in this sample. World Bank figures for Bangladesh in 2008 put gross national income (GNI) per capita at US $520 (World Bank, 2009). Bearing in mind that these are averages, and that within this poor sample there is considerable variation, it is not hard to see why the poor struggle to pay the costs of educating their children.

Figure 3.1 shows the unequal participation of children in education from different income groups. Households which have less than Tk. 2,000 income per month (US $29) are sending almost 25 per cent fewer of their children to school than those who are in the Tk. 8,000 (US $115) and above income group.

In 2007, 5.7 per cent of surveyed children had dropped out of school, and in 2009 this figure stood at 14 per cent. In addition, 8.4 per cent (2007) and 7.5 per cent (2009) of surveyed school age children had never entered school. Rates of dropout and proportions of children who have never been enrolled are inversely correlated to the increase of family income (Figure 3.1). Twelve per cent of children from households living on incomes below Tk. 2,000 per month had never been enrolled in school at all, while a quarter had started school but dropped out. In families earning more than Tk. 8,000 per month meanwhile, 2.6 per cent of children had never been enrolled and 10.6 per cent had dropped out of school. The fact that income is still associated with access to education indicates that policies making education free and compulsory, free school books, along with the government's stipend programmes are not enough to

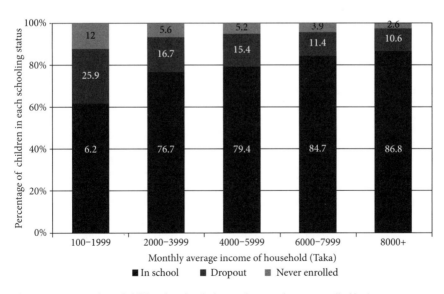

Figure 3.1 Proportion of children in school, dropped out and never enrolled by income group

bring about universal access to primary education. Many of the never-enrolled children were very young; they were within the age range where they were expected to be in school, but had not enrolled yet. So, on-time enrolment is a significant problem that is also associated with poverty. The links between malnutrition, sickness, late enrolment and other forms of exclusion contribute to persistent problems with expanding access to the poorest.

Once poor children get to school, they still face problems getting access to meaningful education. Income was closely correlated with silent exclusion, meaning children who are nominally enrolled but making poor progress or not learning. We identify this form of exclusion with the indicators of children who are attending infrequently, achieving poorly and repeating grades. Silent exclusion is one reason for the poor learning outcomes found in Bangladesh and many other developing countries.

One fifth of primary school-going children were silently excluded, having repeated years of school, having low attainment or irregular attendance. This of course only applies to those enrolled. At primary level, repetition was the major single indicator (13.1 per cent) of silent exclusion (Table 3.2). The problem of children being in the wrong grade for their age, or 'age in grade incongruent', is also one of the major causes of silent exclusion and dropout in education in Bangladesh. At primary level only 31 per cent of children were of the correct age for their grade in the primary grades, with most of the others being over-age (Hossain 2010). The data indicated that there were no statistically significant gender differences in the indicators of silent exclusion or the composite measure.

Table 3.2 Percentages of children at primary level by components of silent exclusion and gender

Components of silent exclusion (in %)	Primary level		
	Boys	**Girls**	**Total**
Low attendance	4.7	3.5	4.1
Low achievement	11.3	8.6	10.0
Repeaters	13.8	12.3	13.1
Silently excluded (zone 3)	23.1	19.7	21.4

These rates of silent exclusion are almost certainly underestimates. Self-reported attendance is more likely to be underreported to enumerators when the expectation is that every child should attend all the time, especially if they qualify for stipends as a result. Self-reported achievement resulted in too few children being classified as low ranking in class (less than 25 per cent said that they were in the bottom 25 per cent). Repetition is also easy to underreport since it can take place several times over several years. This does not reduce the validity of the data collected; it suggests that the problems revealed here might in fact be worse than suspected.

Silently excluded children came from households that had significantly lower incomes than those who were not silently excluded. When we examine the different indicators of silent exclusion separately we see that there was no significant difference in income between high attendees and low attendees. However, the low achievers and grade repeaters in primary and secondary schools come from a significantly lower income group. Children from different socio-economic groups attend more or less equally but achievement levels of the children from low-income groups remain low, and they are more likely to repeat years and become over-age. Repetition and low achievement account for the majority of the pupils counted as silently excluded, which is why the overall relationship between silently exclusion and income poverty is significant. These two aspects of silent exclusion are related since over-age children perform poorly in school. This is why the concepts of silent exclusion and meaningful access are so important. Rates of enrolment and attendance alone do not give an accurate picture of access to education.

Many subtle (and not so subtle) mechanisms in society and schools in Bangladesh mean that the poor are being excluded from school through lack of access to affordable schools, dropping out and being silently excluded. Health and nutritional problems, which are associated with poverty, are one of the most significant of these mechanisms. In the survey data, parents' perception of their children's health is categorized into two groups: 'good health' and 'not so good health'. 'Not so good' health children are those who have been always sick or occasionally sick in the last year according to their parents. In addition, data were collected about whether a child had been sick in the last 30 days. The data show a positive correlation between those with higher incomes and being in the 'good heath' category. Poorer children were more likely to be in the category of children with health problems.

Just over three of the 6–15-year-old children in this sample were suffering from either severe or occasional health problems. Of them, 74.3 per cent were enrolled and 25.7 per cent were out of school (11.4 per cent had dropped out and 14.3 per cent had never enrolled). Among not-sick children in the same age group 12.2 per cent were out of school. This indicates that a large number of children are excluded from basic education due to poor health. Children suffering from health problems were twice as likely as others to be in zones of exclusion 1 and 2 – never enrolled or dropped out of primary school.

To give an indication of the types of health problems suffered by children in rural Bangladesh, Chen et al.'s (1980) large epidemiological study of the causes of children's deaths in rural Bangladesh in the 1970s found that the most significant causes were diarrhoea, tetanus, measles, fever, respiratory disease, drowning, and skin disease (Chen et al. 1980, p. 25). In the 2007 ComSS the most common illnesses reported were coughs (64 per cent), 'weakness' (13 per cent) and hookworm (5 per cent).

The next three sections describe the relationships between exclusion from education in the three zones of exclusion that relate to primary schooling – the never enrolled (zone 1), children who have dropped out (zone 2) and the silently excluded (zone 3) – and indicators of health and nutritional status.

The never enrolled

The ComSS survey focused on children aged 4–15 years old as a reference age group and collected data for the same sample in two rounds. In the ComSS round 1 survey in 2007, of children aged 4–15, 15.9 per cent were never enrolled in any school. Among the 1,406 never-enrolled children aged 4–15 identified in the first round, 875 children (62.2 per cent) had enrolled in the second round. It is important to disaggregate the data by age to understand which children enrolled between the two rounds of data collection and which remained in the category of 'never enrolled'. Tracking never-enrolled children of age 6–10 between rounds shows that 64.5 per cent of these children enrolled by 2009, with more girls enrolled compared to boys. Among the whole sample, more than half of the children aged 6–9 were found not to have enrolled in any school, with the highest figure for children aged 6 (78.7 per cent). This is due to a pattern of late enrolment of children discussed by Hossain (2010).

When parents in the survey of children who had never been to school were asked about the reasons why their children had never been to school, they rarely mentioned health reasons. However, the survey data indicate that the health of never-enrolled children was worse than that of other children. A greater proportion of them were described as being sick or in mediocre health than the enrolled children (Figure 3.2).

In addition to higher rates of sickness (32 per cent rather than 27 per cent were sick in the last 30 days), never-enrolled children had significantly lower

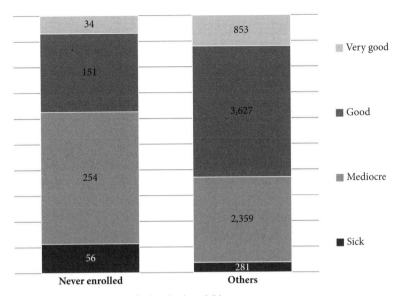

Figure 3.2 Health of never-enrolled and other children

rates of coverage by public health interventions such as immunizations (67 per cent rather than 88 per cent) and visits from health workers (17 per cent rather than 20 per cent). This indicates that the households are marginalized in more ways than one and do not benefit from public health initiatives that have the potential to help them overcome preventable health problems.

Remarkably, never-enrolled children were about two inches shorter than other children on average, controlling for age and sex. This height difference persists throughout the 6–15 age range, suggesting that both low height-for-age and non-enrolment are both caused by a third factor such as poverty. Low height for age is an indicator of stunting, which suggests long-term malnutrition. Malnutrition in early childhood is associated with delayed school enrolment. As discussed above, the data suggest that late enrolment of children in school is very common in this sample and is one of the major causes, along with repetition of the problems, of children becoming over-age in grade (Glewwe and Jacoby 1995; Hossain 2010). Given that many of the never-enrolled children were between the ages of 6 and 9, this indicates that height may be used as an indicator of whether a child is ready to go to school rather than age, which is similar to findings in Ghana (Buxton 2011).

Children who have dropped out from school

Zone 2 includes children who are excluded from education having once attended school. Parents identified these children as 'dropouts' if they had not been to school at all in the last six months. A substantial number of children are excluded from the education system after they are enrolled in school. This group, which includes a larger percentage of boys than girls, is due to a combination of pull-out factors and push-out factors. Pull-out factors include poverty (and related poor health and nutrition), low attendance and involvement of children in income-generating activities. Push-out factors include large classes, lack of teacher attention and care, boring and ineffective teaching and learning practices and low achievement as a result. Dropping out of school is usually the result of a series of factors acting in combination over a period of time; it is a process rather than an event (Hunt 2008). As such it has antecedents which can be identified and which are included in the indicators for zone 3 and discussed in the next section.

The baseline data collected in 2007 from households showed that 5.7 per cent of the sample of all 6–15 years in households who were initially enrolled dropped out from school. The second round data, collected from the same households in 2009, showed a higher dropout rate compared to the first round data – it stood at around 14 per cent, meaning that there was about 2.5 times increase in dropout of over a two-year period. This difference does not seem to be due to naturally occurring factors and is probably a result of differences in reporting between rounds of data collection.

As with the parents of never-enrolled children, the parents of children who had dropped out from school rarely gave poor health as the main reason for dropping out, yet their children had worse health than other children. A significantly smaller proportion of them were categorized as having good or very good health and they had significantly lower rates of immunization (53 per cent had generally good health or very good health rather than 63 per cent of others). Significantly fewer of them had received a complete course of immunizations (68 per cent rather than 88 per cent of other children). However, more of their households had been visited by a health worker (although the causality is hard to establish for this indicator, were they sick because they hadn't been visited or were they visited because they were sick?). Unlike zone 1 children, zone 2 children were not shorter in height than the comparison group.

Sabates et al. (2010) compare the data from the two rounds of the survey to conduct a longitudinal analysis of dropping out from school. Children whose parents reported that their health had improved between the two rounds were less likely to drop out from school. They also found that a higher proportion of children who dropped out were underweight and overweight compared with children who remained in education. Compared to height, weight gives a more temporary indication of poor health or malnutrition, which fits with the two-year time frame of the longitudinal work done by Sabates et al. (2010).

Silently excluded children

About a fifth of children at the primary school level were silently excluded (Table 3.2). They were identified using three indicators of silent exclusion. However, very few children met all three criteria of silent exclusion, with most being defined as silently excluded by one of the indicators alone.

A significant contributing factor to silent exclusion is the prevalence of children who are over-age for their grade. This leads to very wide age ranges in classes and teenagers studying in primary school alongside very young children. These factors cause problems for teachers trying to use a monograde curriculum, which assumes that all the children in a class are of the same age and cognitive level. It also leads to behavioural problems in school. As children get older the opportunity costs of them being in school increase and the likelihood of them dropping out or attending infrequently increases (Lewin 2007). This issue too is related to health and nutritional factors.

Hossain (2010) shows that being in the right age for the grade is associated with the health of the children, especially in the lower grades. Children with 'not so good' health are more likely to be in the wrong age for their grade compared to the children with 'good health'. Children become comparatively more vulnerable to slow progression due to health problems as they progress through the grades. Low height and weight for age (signs of poor nutritional status) are also associated with slow progression through the grades (Hossain 2010, p. 12).

Poor health is associated with being over-age in grade, but also with other aspects of silent exclusion. A significantly higher proportion of children with poor health are present in zone 3 compared to children with good health. Poor health is strongly correlated with all three indicators of silent exclusion (low attainment, low attendance and repetition) (Figure 3.3). Children with low attendance, for

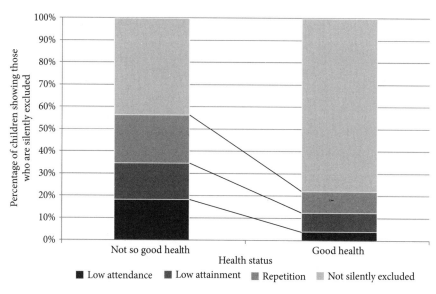

Figure 3.3 Percentages of children by different health status who are silently excluded

example, were significantly less likely to be in good health than the comparison group of enrolled children. Fifty-six per cent of children with low attendance were in 'good health' compared to 65 per cent of the comparison group.

Silent exclusion from education is related to health and nutritional status in several ways. First, it is clear that children who are sick are likely to miss days of school and be categorized as attending infrequently. These children are likely to fall behind with their learning and then to need to repeat grades. Second, the relationship between health and nutrition and issues of late enrolment and grade repetition indicate that health and nutrition are major causes of over-age in grade children in primary schools in Bangladesh, as they are in Ghana (Buxton 2011). Both sets of relationships interact with income poverty to create considerable challenges for the poorest and most vulnerable Bangladeshi children to complete school.

Conclusions

Data from the community and school surveys show clear relationships between poverty and exclusion from education in Bangladesh. These forms of exclusion take effect in different ways. Children from poorer families are less likely to go to school, more likely to drop out of school and even once they are in school are more likely to be 'silently excluded' from education.

Poor health and nutrition are manifestations of poverty, which are closely interrelated with these types of exclusion from education. Children with poor health (which is linked to income and nutrition) perform worse in education than others. The scale and persistence of exclusion from education of poor people in Bangladesh raises questions about policies to improve equity in access to education in Bangladesh. The interrelatedness of these issues suggests that tackling health and nutritional problems alongside problems of educational exclusion is important.

The analysis illustrates several different relationships between poverty, health and exclusion from education. While income poverty is clearly important, the data indicate that among a very poor sample of people, other manifestations of poverty are also important. Income poverty is closely associated with indicators of poor health, (in this case poor self-reported health). This indicator of poor health was strongly and significantly associated with all the different measures of educational exclusion and with the composite measure of all three. Children who were identified as being in poor health by their parents were significantly more likely to have never enrolled in school, to have dropped out of school or to be 'silently excluded'. We can conclude from this analysis that poverty and poor health are major causes of educational exclusion in Bangladesh.

Health problems are linked to nutritional problems as well as public health concerns such as poor hygiene, unclean drinking water, low rates of immunization and parasitic infections. The relationships between poor nutrition and educational access are widely discussed in other literature (such as Grira 2004). These problems can start long before children are of school age and have long-term irreversible consequences for children (Helmers and Patnam 2010). Early childhood care and development (ECCD) is often advocated as the type of intervention that can boost childhood nutrition and help later cognitive development (Nonoyama-Tarumi and Ota 2010). Improving maternal health and the health of babies in their first few years can improve education outcomes later in childhood (Helmers and Patnam 2010). Good childhood health requires interventions that start before birth and continue into adulthood (Bundy et al. 2006).

The data indicate strong relationships between whether a child has completed a full range of immunizations and visits from health workers and the first two zones of exclusion. These associations indicate either that there is a hard core of people who are not able to access both health and education services or that the poor health of children not properly immunized or visited by health workers leads to exclusion from education, or more probably, both.

It indicates the importance of extending immunization drives to the poorest and neediest, and of visits from health workers to poor families. In a similar finding, Sabates et al. (2010) found that visits to households by teachers were associated with lower rates of dropout.

Beyond the effects of poor health and nutrition in delaying children's education, reducing attendance and increasing dropout, the links between education and health are complex and cyclical. Education promotes more healthy behaviour, and leads to greater health for the better educated, their spouses and their children. Education also leads to better economic outcomes, rank in society, social networks and access to information which can all promote health, access to health care and healthy lifestyles (Cutler and Lleras-Muney 2006). Better health leads to more education, but more education also leads to better health.

In practical terms, schools, teachers and education systems are efficient and effective for the delivery of health and nutrition interventions (Bundy et al. 2006). Interventions such as a school-feeding programme might help to incentivize attendance at school for the poorest. If run properly, such a scheme would help to avoid hunger, undernourishment, malnourishment, micronutrient deficiencies and related health problems among children of poor families. Among a host of other benefits, improving attendance, nutritional status and combating hunger would help to increase enrolment, attendance and learning outcomes for children.

Visits by doctors or local health workers to schools to check on children, and monitor indicators of their health and development would help to identify nutritional and health problems. This could also help with the identification of poor families who qualify for conditional cash transfer programmes. Few of the schools in the school survey had any facilities to treat sick children, organized student health care systems, or student health records.

Raising awareness of poverty-related exclusion and health and nutrition issues and training teachers to identify children at risk of exclusion due to poverty would be a way of avoiding some of these problems, increasing the positive long-term effects of education on health outcomes and helping with targeting of interventions. Teachers could be trained as part of teacher training to watch out for signs of malnutrition (such as under height and weight), identify common illnesses, identify children who do not have proper school equipment, who have to work or are from landless families.

More broadly, this chapter indicates that there are many complex links between educational exclusion and health and nutritional status. The aims expressed in the MDGs of improving maternal health, eradicating hunger and achieving universal primary education cannot be pursued independently. There are many ways in the short term and in the long term in which achieving one cannot be achieved without the others, and in which progress towards one goal will help to achieve the others.

Questions for reflection

- Why might children from less well-educated households have worse health in developed as well as developing countries?
- How are health and nutritional problems endogenous to other indicators and manifestations of poverty such as exclusion from education?
- What cost-effective measures can schools take to improve the health of children and promote healthy lifestyles?
- How might health, nutrition and education goals be tackled together in developing country contexts such as Bangladesh in the post 2015 development agenda?

Acknowledgements

This chapter uses data from the Consortium for Research on Educational Access, Transitions and Equity's (CREATE) research in Bangladesh, which was funded by the Department for International Development. A team from BRAC University's Institute of Education Development led by Altaf Hossain and Dr Manzoor Ahmed carried out the survey. We are grateful to Professor Keith Lewin, Dr Ricardo Sabates and Dr Stuart Cameron, as well as the anonymous peer reviewer for their help with earlier versions of this chapter.

Further reading

1. Khanam, R., Nghiem, H. S. and Rahman, M. M. (2011) The Impact of Childhood Malnutrition on Schooling: Evidence from Bangladesh, *Journal of Biosocial Science*, 43: 437–451.

   and

2. Grira, H. (2004) The Determinants of Grade Attainment in Low-Income Countries: Evidence from Rural Bangladesh, *The Developing Economies*, XLII-4 (December 2004): 494–509.

These papers are particularly useful due to the range of determinants covered and the sophisticated analysis of data on nutrition and education. Unlike other research, they control for the endogeneity of nutritional problems when analysed alongside other variables – meaning that the problems may be so closely interrelated that it is difficult to tell which is the cause and which the effect or analyse them independently. These papers provide a strong case for the importance of nutrition on education and provide good explanatory context to understanding the causes of the huge problem of over-age children in many developing countries' education systems.

3. Hossain, A. (2010) *Age in Grade Congruence and Progression in Basic Education in Bangladesh*, CREATE Pathways to Access, Research Monograph, No. 48. University of Sussex: Centre for International Education, Brighton, UK.

This paper develops the issue of age in grade with a detailed account of the relationships between age in grade, health and poverty. The scale and effects of the problems discussed surrounding age in grade are very revealing in terms of understand the challenges of delivering quality education for all in developing countries and the inefficiency of many education systems.

4. Pridmore, P. (2007) *Impact of Health on Education Access and Achievement: A Cross-National Review of the Research Evidence*, CREATE Pathways to Access, Research Monograph No 2, Institute of Education, University of London, London, UK.

This paper is very useful as it provides an accessible but rigorous review of the issues and literature on the links between health and education. It is accessible in that it is free to access online, and summarizes material well for non-experts. It provides in one place a good overview of the wide ranging literature and its findings about the complex and interlinked relationships between health and nutrition.

References

Ahmed, M., (2011). *The Sector-wide Approach in Bangladesh Primary Education: A Critical View, CREATE Pathways to Access Research Monograph No. 57*. Dhaka: BRAC.

—— (2011). *Trade-off between Child Labour and Schooling in Bangladesh: Role of Parental Education, Monash University Department of Economics Discussion paper 21/11*, Melbourne: Monash University.

Ahmed, M., Ahmed, K. S., Khan, N. I. and Ahmed, R. (2007). *Access to Education in Bangladesh: Country Analytic Review of Primary and Secondary School*, CREATE Country Analytic Review. Dhaka/Brighton: BU-IED/ University of Sussex.

Ahmed, M., Nath, S. R., Hossain, A., Kabir, M., Kalam, A., Shahjamal, M., Yasmin, R. N. and Zafar, T. (2005). *Quality with Equity: The Primary Education Agenda, Education Watch 2004*. Bangladesh: Campaign for Popular Education (CAMPE).

Ahmad, Q. K., Ahmed, K. S., Islam, M. S., Sinha, N. C., Banu, N., Majumder, M. H. K., Ullah, S. S. H. and Sultana, M. M. (2007). *Financing Primary and Secondary Education in Bangladesh, Education Watch 2006*. Bangladesh: Campaign for Popular Education (CAMPE).

Al-Samarrai, S. (2009). The impact of governance on education inequality: evidence from Bangladesh. *Public Administration and Development, 29*(3): 167–179.

Arends-Kuenning, M. and Amin, S. (2004). School incentive programs and children's activities: the case of Bangladesh. *Comparative Education Review, 48*(3): 295–317.

Asadullah, M. N. and Chaudhury, N. (2009). Reverse gender gap in schooling in Bangladesh: insights from urban and rural households. *Journal of Development Studies*, 45(8): 1360–1380.

Baulch, B. (2010). *The Medium-Term Impact of the Primary Education Stipend in Rural Bangladesh, IFPRI Discussion Paper 00976*, Washington: International Food Policy Research Institute.

Bundy, D. A. P., Shaeffer, S., Jukes, M., Beegle, K., Gillespie, A., Drake, L., Frances Lee, S., Hoffman, A., Jones, J., Mitchell, A., Barcelona, D., Camara, B., Golmar, C., Saviloli, L., Sembene, M., Takeuchi, T. and Wright, C. (2006). School-Based Health and Nutrition Programs. In Jamison, D. T., Breman, J. G., Measham, A. R., Alleyne, G., Claeson, M., Evans, D. B., Jha, P., Mills, A. and Musgrove, P. (Eds). *Disease Control Priorities in Developing Countries*, 2nd ed. New York: Oxford University Press, 1091–1108.

Buxton, C. (2011). *The Impact of Malnutrition on Access to Primary Education: Case Studies from Ghana, CREATE Pathways to Access, Research Monograph, No. 68*. University of Sussex: Centre for International Education/University of Cape Coast: Brighton, UK/Cape Coast, Ghana.

Chen, L. C., Rahman, M. and Sarder, A. M. (1980). Epidemiology and causes of death among children in a rural area of Bangladesh. *International Journal of Epidemiology*, 9(1): 25–33.

Choe, C., Dzhumashev, R., Islam, A. and Khan, Z. A. (2013). The effect of informal networks on corruption in education: Evidence from the household survey data in Bangladesh. *Journal of Development Studies*, 49(2): 238–250.

Cutler, D. M. and Llera-Muney, A. (2006). *Education and Health: Evaluating Theories and Evidence, National Bureau of Economic Research Working Paper 12352*, Cambridge MA, National Bureau of Economic Research.

Deolalikar, A. B. (2005). Poverty and child malnutrition in Bangladesh. *Journal of Developing Societies*, 21(1–2): 55–90.

Driessen, J., Razzaque, A., Walker, D. and Canning, D. (2011). The effect of childhood measles vaccination on school enrollment in Matlab, Bangladesh, *PGDA Working Paper No. 81, Program on the Global Demography of Aging Working Paper Series*, Cambridge, MA: Harvard Initiative for Global Health.

Filmer, D. and Pritchett, L. H. (2001). Estimating wealth effects without expenditure data – of TEARS: an application to educational enrollments in states of India. *Demography*, 38(1): 115–132.

Glewwe, P. and Jacoby, H. G. (1995). An economic analysis of delayed primary-school enrolment in a low-income country: the role of early childhood nutrition. *Review of Economics and Statistics*, 77(1): 156–169.

Grira, H. (2004). The determinants of grade attainment in low-income countries: Evidence from rural Bangladesh. *The Developing Economies*, 42(4): 494–509

Helmers, C. and Patnam, M. (2010). The formation and evolution of childhood skill acquisition: evidence from India. *Journal of Development Economics*, 95(2): 252–266.

Hossain, A. (2010). *Age in Grade Congruence and Progression in Basic Education in Bangladesh*, CREATE Pathways to Access, Research Monograph, No. 48. University of Sussex: Centre for International Education, Brighton, UK.

Hossain, A. and Zeitlyn, B. (2010). *Poverty and Equity: Access to Education in Bangladesh*, CREATE Pathways to Access Research Monograph No. 51. Dhaka/Brighton: BRAC/University of Sussex.

Hossain, N. (2010). School Exclusion as Social Exclusion: the Practices and Effects of a Conditional Cash Transfer Programme for the Poor in Bangladesh, *Journal of Development Studies*, 46(7): 1264–1282.

Hunt, F. (2008). *Dropping Out from School: A Cross Country Review of the Literature. CREATE Pathways to Access Research Monograph No. 16*. Brighton: University of Sussex.

Khanam, R., Nghiem, H. S. and Rahman, M. M. (2011). The impact of childhood malnutrition on schooling: evidence from Bangladesh. *Journal of Biosocial Science*, 43(4): 437–451.

Lewin, K. M. (2007). *Improving Access, Equity and Transitions in Education: Creating a Research Agenda, CREATE Pathways to Access, Research Monograph No 1*. Brighton: University of Sussex.

Nonoyama-Tarumi, Y. and Y. Ota (2010). Early childhood development in developing countries: pre-primary education, parenting, and health care. *Background paper for the EFA Global Monitoring Report 2011*. Paris: United Nations Educational, Scientific and Cultural Organization (UNESCO).

Pridmore, P. (2007). *Impact of Health on Education Access and Achievement: A Cross-National Review of the Research Evidence*, CREATE Pathways to Access, Research Monograph No 2, University of London: Institute of Education, London, UK.

Raynor, J. and Wesson, K. (2006). The girls' stipend program in Bangladesh. *Journal of Education for International Development* 2(2), Available at: http://www.equip123.net/JEID/articles/3/Girls'StipendPrograminBangladesh.pdf (accessed 8 July 2010).

Sabates, R., Hossain, A. and Lewin, K. M. (2010). *School Drop Out in Bangladesh: New Insights from Longitudinal Evidence* CREATE Pathways to Access Research Monograph No. 48. Dhaka/Brighton: BRAC/University of Sussex.

Tarleton, J. L., Haque, R., Mondal, D., Shu, J., Farr, B. M. and Petri, W. A. (2006). Cognitive effects of diarrhea, malnutrition, and entamoeba histolytica infection on school age children in Dhaka, Bangladesh. *American Journal of Tropical Medicine and Hygiene*, 74(3): 475–481.

Tietjen, K. (2003). The Bangladesh primary education stipend project: A descriptive analysis: World Bank, Available at: http://siteresources.worldbank.org/EDUCATION/Resources/278200-1099079877269/547664-1099080014368/BangladeshStipend.pdf (accessed 12 August 2010)

World Bank (2008). Education for All in Bangladesh: Where does Bangladesh stand in achieving the EFA goals by 2015? Bangladesh Development Series, Paper No. 24.

———, (2009). Bangladesh at a glance, statistics, Available at: http://devdata.worldbank.org/AAG/bgd_aag.pdf (accessed 12 August 2010).

The Impact of the Haitian Earthquake on a Fragile Education System

Helena Murseli and Naoko Imoto

4

Introduction

On 12 January 2010, an earthquake of the unprecedented magnitude of 7.0 hit the Haitian capital of Port-au-Prince, causing more than 220,000 deaths, many of whom were school children. More than 4,000 schools with vulnerable structures were destroyed or severely damaged. The already fragile education sector was almost entirely destroyed, while the Ministry of National Education and Vocational Training (MENFP) lost its building and some of the highest-level staff (MENFP 2010).

Within a few weeks, massive assistance started arriving from all over the world. Seeing the devastating images of collapsed buildings, many people thought of the need to rebuild schools and to bring children back to school in one of the world's poorest countries. Around 200 agencies, including non-governmental, religious and United Nations (UN) organizations, gathered to provide educational assistance on the ground. Many of them had very little information upon their arrival, where they were encountered by massive piles of debris, tents in every vacant land and on streets and no credible list of schools existed.

Three months after the earthquake, in April 2010, thousands of school children in the affected area returned to schools made of makeshift tarpaulins. By the end of 2010, it was proved that almost 100 per cent of school-going children have returned to school (Education Cluster 2011), and around 72 per cent of children living in camps were in school (Education Cluster 2010).

This chapter intends to present how humanitarian assistance helped to recover the education sector and reduce vulnerability in post-earthquake Haiti despite numerous challenges. It also aims to describe the pre- and post-earthquake situations on how, despite the strong commitment of the government to address the main barriers related to access to education, structural issues and patterns are weakly tackled to allow all children in Haiti to benefit from a quality education and sustainably acquire basic learning competencies and skills that enable them to contribute to the development of their communities and society.

Before the earthquake

With 78 per cent of its citizens living on less than two dollars a day, Haiti remains not merely the poorest country in the Western Hemisphere but also one of the most unequal (UNDP 2007). Small elites of no more than several thousand families are extremely wealthy, while an estimated 80 per cent of Haitians live in absolute poverty. Statistics suggest that the richest 10 per cent of Haitians receive nearly 48 per cent of the nation's income, while the poorest 10 per cent receive less than 0.9 per cent. A child born in the poorest quintiles has 50 per cent fewer chances to reach his fifth birthday than a child born in the top quintile (UNDP 2007).

Inequity also persists in the education sector: before the earthquake, less than half of children on average were in school and only one third completed primary compulsory education with huge geographical disparities. While three out of four children in urban areas started primary schooling, only around a half of the children living in rural areas were given this opportunity (MSPP, 2006).

Poverty levels were reflected in completion rates as well; compared to 89 per cent completing primary school in the top quintile born in 1980–1984, only 30 per cent of those in the poorest quintile completed primary education. In secondary school, 70 per cent from the top quintiles complete, compared to just 12 per cent from the lowest quintile (Demombynes et al. 2010). This is partly because many parents marginally generate school fees from meagre income and can afford school fees only irregularly, leaving children frequently absent in school, and eventually causing dropout. Although most Haitians believe that education can offer a hope of moving out of poverty, school has been out of reach for many children of poor families.

One of the biggest bottlenecks in low enrolment and completion is the fact that the majority of schools are private; only 10 per cent of schools were government-owned before the earthquake, imposing burdens of school fees and other indirect education costs on extremely poor families living on less than two dollars a day (MENFP 2010). Historically, the Haitian government has made very low public expenditure on education, approximately 5 per cent in 2007 (Demombynes et al. 2010), leaving many areas without public schools. A huge demand on education, however, created many private and community schools especially in urban areas, and over half of the primary schools were concentrated in Western and Artibonite Departments. Thus, education became out of reach for the poorest families. Approximately 145 sub-communes out of 550 did not have public schools and 23 did not have any education infrastructure, either public or private (MENFP 2010). Even if there is a public school in the community, some children were still left out of school because the parents claimed other costs such as bags, shoes, textbooks and stationery as the main reason for not sending their children to school.

Another challenge of the Haitian education system is a lack of regulation and supervision by the public sector. Out of 88 per cent of non-public schools in the country, only 8 per cent of them function with a licence, a government credential which certifies that minimum facility and quality standards are met (MENFP 2012). The quality of private schools varies; top schools in the country are private with high tuition fees, while the majority of schools operate without proper teaching and learning conditions. Moreover, 59 per cent of urban and 67 per cent of rural schools had no water (MENFP 2012a). Some rudimentary education is offered by church and other charitable organizations, but the quality control of education by the state is meagre, or non-existent. Illiteracy is estimated at over half of the adult population. The difference in licensing between urban and rural areas reinforces the geographical differences in schooling: 17 per cent of the schools located in urban areas were licensed, compared to only 3 per cent of rural schools (MENFP 2012a). This is also a reflection of MENFP's weak presence outside of Haiti's urban areas.

The third challenge of the Haitian education system is a massive proportion of over-aged children in schools. While the mandated age for entering grade one is six years old, the actual mean age is nearly ten, and students in grade six were on average almost 16 (i.e. five years older than expected) (Demombynes et al. 2010). In 2005, a large proportion of older children were attending pre-school: 33 per cent of children aged eight, 17 per cent aged ten and 8 per cent of those aged 12. Likewise, 57 per cent of 16 year olds and almost one-third of 18 year olds were attending primary school. Fifty-four per cent of schools were 'multigrade,' having more than one grade in the same classroom. Teachers without training and proper skills with multi-age classrooms face the challenge of adapting teaching methods to satisfy the interests and attention needs of children of different age groups at the same time, thus contributing to poor student performance. It can also contribute significantly to the increase of the dropout rate, as demonstrated by the study on Out-of-School Children undertaken by UNICEF/UNESCO Institute of Statistics (2009).

All of the challenges aforementioned are imposed on teachers in schools, majority of whom are unqualified and untrained. Less than 12 per cent of 70,000 registered teachers in primary education meet the required qualifications to teach, and the rest received little or no training, facing heavy burdens of the poor environment without proper spaces, teaching and learning materials, uneven level of multigrade students and poor attendance (MENFP, 2012a).

Needless to say, this exacerbates inefficiency and results in very poor quality education with low learning achievements. Early grade reading assessment in two regions conducted in 2008 and 2009 showed 29 per cent of third graders, who participated in the Creole assessment could not read a single word of connected text (World Bank, 2009). According to the education census for 2010–2011, only 11.2 per cent in public and 11.6 per cent in private schools of the 70,000 registered teachers in primary education completed the necessary studies required to teach (MENFP 2012a, See Figure 4.1).

All these factors result in poor learning, attendance, dropout and non-enrolment of the most vulnerable children, including those with poor nutrition and health, disabled children or orphans. Children were also deemed to be extremely vulnerable to violence, exploitation and abuse. Heavy rains and natural disasters are also regular phenomenon, which disturb schooling.

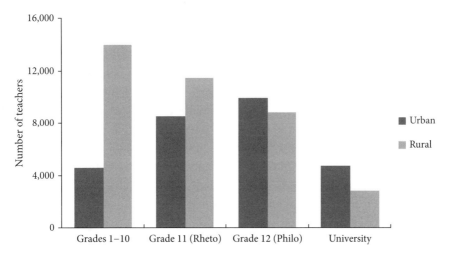

Figure 4.1 Teachers according to level of education

Source: United Nations Office for the Coordination of Humanitarian Affairs (OCHA) (2010), *Flash Appeal: Haiti Humanitarian Appeal (Revised) (January–December 2010)*, Available at: http://fts.unocha.org/reports/daily/ocha_R32sum_A893___19_November_2013_(03_01).pdf

As described, the pre-earthquake Haiti saw almost a half of children out of school, and a near anarchic school system before the January 2010 earthquake devastated the sector.

The earthquake emergency response and transition to recovery

For children and people among the poorest of the Haitian population, the magnitude 7.0 earthquake on 12 January 2010 was beyond overwhelming. In particular, the education sector was one of the hardest hit. Property damage, loss of life and psychological trauma on children and teachers were enormous. The MENFP's central structure was strongly shaken by the collapse of a large part of the building that housed the technical directorates. Nearly 4,000 schools, or 90 per cent of schools in the affected area, were destroyed or severely damaged, including over 77 per cent of existing public infrastructures. More than 2.5 million children saw their school year interrupted (MENFP 2010).

Within a week, overwhelming and massive support was poured into Haiti by numerous organizations and individuals around the world to respond to the immediate needs of the earthquake victims. This included massive assistance to help rebuild the education sector. For many people, a humanitarian response means immediate life-saving activities such as health, water and food. Education can often be seen as part of the recovery and reconstruction process, even by fellow humanitarian workers. However, education opportunities lost in natural and man-made disasters can actually be life threatening. Education at the time of emergencies and post-emergencies provides physical, psychosocial and cognitive protection that can be life sustaining and life saving. It offers the ability to identify and provide support for affected individuals, particularly children and youth, and also mitigates the psychosocial impact on disasters by giving a sense of normalcy, stability, structure and hope for the future. Education provides knowledge and skills to survive in a crisis through life-saving information such as disaster prevention and hygiene. It can also build social capital and enhances social cohesion, contributing to stability of societies (The Inter-Agency Network for Education in Emergencies (INEE) Minimum Standards 2010).

A total of USD 86,271,684 was collected for the education sector in 2010 according to the centralized tracking system administered by UN Office of Coordination for Humanitarian Affairs (OCHA), but this excludes much more aid brought by individuals and numerous missionary organizations, among others, which operate independently (OCHA 2010). Thus, aid needed to be coordinated so as to make sure that all needs were efficiently covered without much duplication and urgent response was delivered.

In the view of enhancing efficiency in humanitarian emergency response, the UN and other humanitarian organizations set up a mechanism of predictable leadership and more effective coordination called the Cluster system in 2007 (Inter-Agency Standing Committee 2006). This system was applied immediately after the earthquake in Haiti; two weeks after the quake, the Education Cluster became rapidly functional and started coordinating around 200 local and international organizations, aiming to improve efficiency in aid efforts, provide technical, material and financial support to the government and all partners.

The first step was to gather as many education partners on the ground as possible to create a coordination platform. The Minimum Standards for Education in Emergencies put together by the Inter-Agency Network for Education in Emergencies (INEE) were disseminated among partners as the guiding principles to make sure that the relief efforts were streamlined based on international norms and standards, in such areas as school construction, safety and psychosocial aspects. This helped organizations that had not been familiar with educational emergency assistance.

A significant component of the Cluster coordination function relied on its information management system. All partners were asked to report activities using the common format called 4Ws (Who, What, Where, When) to help partners to avoid duplication, improve efficiency in finding gaps and find other partners that are doing the same intervention to learn lessons. This also helped to make an overall view of the aid efforts, finding overall progress and gaps in physical and financial resources, making it easier to regularly report back to donors and to raise further funds. A joint comprehensive multi-sector assessment was also conducted, and produced the list of damaged schools – a significant piece of information where there had been no list of schools in the country before the earthquake.

In fact, to coordinate various actors with different issues and needs in a speedy manner was difficult. The strategic group was formed with representatives of larger non-governmental organizations (NGOs), both national and international, and UN organizations. Furthermore, to enhance more specific decision-making in each theme, the Thematic Working Groups were established to coordinate different activities such as reconstruction, teacher training, psychosocial support and early childhood education. Each group shared experiences, and set norms and standards. For example, designs and specifications for temporary learning spaces were discussed and shared. Teaching manuals for psychosocial support were disseminated for other organizations to replicate. Debris removal from school premises was coordinated with some contingents of the United Nations Peace Keeping Operation so that spaces were cleared for temporary learning.

In April 2010, three months after the quake, a massive 'Back to School' initiative was organized by MENFP, supported by education partners to re-open schools. A total of 1,600 tents were provided to set up more than 225 temporary learning spaces, while overall efforts helped 600 schools to reopen with distributions of learning materials and school equipment benefiting more than 325,000 children and 42,000 teachers (Education Cluster 2010). The World Food Programme ensured food for all children in schools and inter-sectorial approach was promoted to provide water and sanitation services as well as protection, especially psycho-social support to children affected by the earthquake. Around 4,000 affected schools received subsidies by the World Bank's Education for All programme to help the infrastructure and to reduce the burdens of potential increase on school fees (although the impact of these subsidies was not found because of lack of monitoring and evaluation). These efforts not only helped minimize disruption of schooling since the earthquake, but also gave a huge relief for Haitians.

Another massive 'Go to School' initiative was organized for the new school year in October 2010, targeting 720,000 children nationwide (out of 2.2 million primary school age children at national level, with more than half out of school), 15,000 teachers and 2,000 schools in all ten departments, reaching 80 per cent of those children directly affected by the earthquake, with efforts coordinated with all education partners. Vulnerable and poorest children were provided with school material, Early Childhood Development kits while education staff were trained on psycho-social care, and 4,000 tents were set up to host temporary learning spaces and semi-permanent schools were being built (Education Cluster 2011).

However, while Haitian people were slowly recovering from the devastating earthquake, another crisis hit the country a few months later, which brought a new challenge to the humanitarian aid and the Haitian government to help people and bring relief. The cholera disease, which was found in October in the Artibonite region, spread all over the country in a few weeks. For school-going children and teachers, this was especially life-threatening as most schools do not have proper water and sanitation facilities to prevent children from cholera disease. The cholera crisis, as well as the hurricanes and political unrest that followed, was a constant reminder to all humanitarian actors of the fragile situation and the weak education system. The confluence of crises, associated with a significant decrease of the humanitarian funding, had significantly amplified the complexity and the difficulties of the humanitarian response. Yet again, the education partners coordinated activities in schools such as distributing hygiene-promotion materials and teaching children the importance of hand-washing. Cholera prevention and response were massively organized in schools, and emergency preparedness and response contributed to capacity-building activities.

Despite many challenges, a large proportion of the emergency resources poured into the education sector were coordinated to an extent, and many school children received support to go back to school. A report jointly produced by the Education and Camp Coordination and Camp Management (CCCM) Clusters in November 2010 indicated that 72 per cent of girls and boys aged 6–14 that lived in camps were enrolled in school (Education Cluster 2010). Compared to the pre-earthquake figure of primary enrolment for Metropolitan Port-au-Prince, this was an encouraging mark, especially as many people believed that children in camps must have been left out of school due to the difficulties faced. After the first phase of re-opening schools with tarpaulins, over 500 schools were rebuilt in semi-permanent or permanent structures within 2011 (Education Cluster 2012). In 2012, the Demographic Health Survey (DHS) showed an outstanding increase in primary school enrolment with 78 per cent, compared to the previous score of 48 per cent in 2007 (MSPP 2012). Overall, it is perhaps not exaggerating to say that the emergency response had an impact on repairing and reconstructing school infrastructure, providing psychosocial support and reducing some financial burdens covered by mass school material distribution.

However, it is questionable to what extent the post-earthquake aid contributed to bring out-of-school children back to school as the majority of aid was delivered at school level. Even if non-public schools received subsidies, it might have been used for repairing infrastructure, and not enough evidence was seen for decrease of school fees to reduce financial burdens on families. This was one of the biggest challenges and dilemma facing the humanitarian partners. There were not enough activities for out-of-school children, except for few agencies working in camps for non-formal education. In fact, school fees remained as a major barrier to school attendance in the system in which 80 per cent of education is provided by the non-public sector (MENFP 2010), and the relentless economic challenges facing the majority of families left many children out of school.

In October 2010, the Interim Haiti Recovery Commission approved the 2010–2015 Operational Plan presented by MENFP. Haiti's international partners, including Canada, the European Union, the Inter-American Development Bank, Japan, Switzerland, the United States, the United Nations and the World Bank have committed over USD $850 million in the education sector for this period (MENFP 2012b).

Current situation and prospect towards development

Strategy and operational plan ready for implementation

The current education situation in Haiti has impressively improved after the earthquake. While in 2007, the DHS reported a Net Attendance Rate of 49 per cent – with huge disparities according to the economic and poverty quintiles (31 per cent from the lowest quintile and 76 per cent for the highest) – in 2012, the most recent DHS shows an important increase up to 77 per cent. Yet the private sector is still predominant (88 per cent) as shown in the last school census published by the Ministry of Education in January 2012. The census counts a total of 16,072 schools for the ten geographical divided education departments and 49 per cent of non-public schools and only 8 per cent of public schools are located in rural areas (MSPP 2012).

Thus inequity still prevails as children from the lowest quintiles have less access to education while the quality of education is still challenging and needs strong investment from the government to recruit and train qualified teachers. There is also a lack of quality control and standards on learning and teaching conditions and material as almost 88 per cent of schools are private (92 per cent of which operate without certificate), negatively impacting children learning outcomes. Repetition rate is still high, as of 15 per cent at primary level (MENFP 2012a).

Nevertheless, the government has shown a strong will to improve the education sector and enable all children to have access to quality education. Immediately after the earthquake, the government had set up a task force to analyse the education situation and define the strategy and plan to be developed during the next five years. The task force was comprised of donors, NGO partners and the Ministry of Education. The 'Operational Plan 2010–2015' elaborated by this task force outlines the roadmap for the stakeholders for the education sector and the priorities determined by the government. It includes the whole education system sectors from pre-school to higher education including governance, budget planning, monitoring and evaluation. The operational plan lies on the Bernard Reform endorsed in 1998 as defined in the 'Training and Education National Plan', followed by the 'Education National Strategy' developed in 2007.

Based on a comprehensive situation analysis of the education sector and its diagnosis before and after the earthquake, the Operational Plan (MENFP 2010) is articulated around nine components: (i) governance, (ii) curricula, (iii) educations staff training, (iv) early childhood and development, and access to compulsory and free primary education, (v) secondary education, (vi) vocational teaching, (vii) higher education, (viii) special needs education and (ix) literacy. Initiated in 2010, this plan was only endorsed by the Ministry of Education and the Local Education Group in 2012. To develop the objectives and implement the activities proposed in the Operational Plan, the Ministry of Education under the leadership of the technical departments, in close cooperation with the donors, put in place technical working groups, according to the nine components with the aim of harmonizing and coordinating the strategies developed for each component and its implementation phases, making sure that all needs are analysed and covered. However, at the time of the mid-term review of the plan, it was reported that only 10 per cent of objectives have been achieved. Much effort has been put into the improvement of governance, school construction, the free education programme (PSUGO) and teacher training.

A School-fee abolition programme to improve access for the poorest children

Elected in April 2011, President Martelly declared education as a high priority for the government, especially access for all children, particularly the poorest. He quickly launched the ambitious Free, Compulsory and Universal Education Programme (PSUGO) in October 2011, a programme managed directly by the government through a special committee and implemented by the Ministry of Education.

Around 500,000 school-aged children have been counted as out-of-school by the government, out of 2.2 million school-aged children, according to the 2012 School Census. Yet, evidence shows that this number may be under-estimated as some marginalized and vulnerable children including disabled and orphaned children may have not been counted. Over-aged children are incredibly numerous in the Haitian education system; representing 65 per cent of children attending school either because they enrol late or have high repetition rates with high risks of dropping out (MENFP 2012c). This also means that over-aged children may be out of school and illiterate. According to the 2007 DHS (MSPP 2012), 47 per cent of school-aged children were never in school, 63 per cent of them were from the lowest quintile and 33 per cent from the highest quintile. The proportion of out-of-school children in 2005 was 45, 5 per cent of school-aged children and 68 per cent of them were from the lowest quintile.

To address the issue of access to education for the poorest children, the government decided to launch an initiative for the abolition of the school fees and support schools by allocating subsidies based on the number of children.

The PSUGO programme (MENFP 2012) targets the poorest children and poorest geographical areas where public and non-public schools are located and where school fees have been determined as an important barrier for access. Indeed, families whose children are not attending school present cost as the main reason. The programme aims at abolishing school fees for about one million children in the ten geographically divided departments of the country, targeting both out-of-school children (never in schools or dropped out of school) and children attending public schools in the most remote areas.

The government plan is to support schools by giving per capita–based subsidies to compensate for parents' fees contribution. The amount of the subsidy, initially 100 gourdes per child (around 2.50 US dollars), was then increased up to 250 gourdes (around 6 US dollars). The programme targets not only public schools but vulnerable non-public schools are also benefitting from it. It is important to note that at its initial stage, the school fees abolition initiative resulted from a very innovative Public-Private Partnership, through US $0.05/minute surtax on inbound international calls to Haiti, and US $1.5 surtax on international wire transfers. The main objective is to lessen the financial barrier determined as one of the most important reasons for children not attending school or dropping out and to alleviate families' financial burden.

In the first year, the programme targeted children in such situations:

1. Children identified as out-of-school aged from 6 to 12 in eight departments (out of ten);
2. Children attending first grade in two vulnerable departments (West and Artibonite);
3. Children attending public schools;
4. Per capita subsidies to most vulnerable non-public schools;
5. Children benefiting from subsidies donated by members of parliament and senators.

The PSUGO was rapidly launched right on time for the school year 2011–2012, although the needs assessment prior to the subsidies transfer to schools was still ongoing. The aim was to encourage parents to send their children to schools by abolishing school fees and also distributing school material, and thus increasing access to education for those children whose parents could not pay direct schooling costs. New classrooms had to be created to welcome children enrolling for the first time and teachers had to be recruited as well to avoid over-crowded classrooms. Field visits conducted by the Ministry of Education and partners during the school year, however, proved the inefficiency of the programme in some education departments due to a lack of preparedness, adequate learning and teaching conditions and sufficient material. School directors and teachers were complaining because they had not been paid for months or received no salary at all from the beginning of the school year. The subsidies promised by the government were not allocated to all targeted schools and as parents were not paying school fees, running costs were drastically missing to allow the school to perform with a minimum of quality. An assessment of the programme was conducted by the Ministry of Education in July 2012. It reports that all children targeted have been reached by the programme and even more children have been enrolled, increasing considerably the attendance rate (MENFP 2012b).The report also indicates that, if families do not pay for school fees, which is the main objective of the programme, schools have less funds for functioning, as promised per capita subsidies have not been paid on time to schools. Teachers are quite often not paid and very often not motivated. The equation seems difficult to be solved: free education for all is right but funding allocation to compensate the abolition of the school fees is not yet efficient. Retention and completion are still to be verified and the impact of the programme on quality and learning achievements is ambivalent. Furthermore, in order to attain its objectives to facilitate universal access to quality basic education with this School Fees Abolition Programme, the government of Haiti and its partners need to undertake several steps that should include:

- Having a good assessment of the sector and a sound monitoring and evaluation plans and processes;
- Planning for quality improvement, and introducing the prioritization of targeted groups, based on level of poverty and vulnerability;
- Strengthening the forecast of additional required inputs (classrooms, teachers, teaching and learning material, among others) and have a broader funding scheme that goes beyond the public-private partnership (including using the fiscal space of the government of Haiti and projecting predictable funding from the international partners);
- Seizing this opportunity to increase government regulatory role, mainly starting from the schools that are already receiving the subsidies and also to use this process as an excellent opportunity to reinforce transparency and accountability throughout the education system.

Conclusion

Overall, the journey of the humanitarian response in the education sector in the aftermath of the January 2010 earthquake in Haiti has shown the effective application of some of the international humanitarian principles, in particular the coordination mechanism for humanitarian assistance. The coordinated response has demonstrated the importance of accountability, leadership, joint and transparent fund raising as well as setting norms and standards and undertaking actions to reduce vulnerability.

These efforts enhanced effective delivery and maximized the impact of the resources collected. Coordinated assistance reached hundreds of school-going children, recovering the sector back to the pre-earthquake level.

However, the education emergency response has also shown that these principles and mechanisms need to be further reinforced and made more flexible to fully respond to the fragile contexts of Haiti, characterized by a very limited government capacity, an extensive chronic and structural poverty, confluence and recurrence of emergencies, as well as unpredictable funding. The question of a swift transition process from humanitarian to recovery and to development-oriented action is also another area that needs to be examined further, and where the guidelines and principles need to be improved, given the fact that in most cases, crises have only exacerbated issues that are deeply rooted in poverty and failure of good governance.

Questions for reflection

1. With the humanitarian assistance given to Haiti, how is it possible to 'build back' given the inherent weak situation of – particularly in this case – the education sector? How do we take into consideration the dangers of building a completely new system and how do we take into account the already existing system in line with the desire to rebuild?
2. Humanitarian aid in the context of Haiti (after the 2010 earthquake), where almost everything has been destroyed, poses the question of the limit of aid in terms of reconstruction and support to the poorest. Particularly for education, when should aid stop?
3. How can one advance and determine norms and standards for the dominated non-public education sector (i.e. schools) in Haiti while at the same time promoting better access for the poorest?

Acknowledgement

The authors would like to thank Mohammed Fall for the substantial input to this chapter.

Further reading

1. Altinok, N. (2010). *Do School Resources Increase School Quality?* Dijon France: IREDU.

This work analyses the effect of resources on school quality and questions the correlation between educational inputs and the education outputs. As relevant to Haiti where the private sector is predominant with variable inputs, and with very poor resources in remote areas.

2. Lunde, H. (2008). *Youth and Education in Haiti, Disincentives, Vulnerabilities and Constraints*. Oslo: Fafo.

   This text presents a study on children attendance, retention and achievement of students in the Haitian context before the earthquake. It analyses the link between poverty and education schooling and presents the strong education demand from the community and how parents struggle to cope with the education-related expenses.

3. Walker, M. (2012). *A Capital or Capabilities Education Narrative in a World of Staggering Inequalities?* Bloemfontein, South Africa: University of the Free State.

   This paper analyses inequities and how education can impact on human capital and human capabilities.

References

Demombynes, G., Holland, P. and Leone, G. (2010), *Students and the Market for Schools in Haiti*, Available at: http://elibrary.worldbank.org/content/workingpaper/10.1596/1813-9450-5503 (accessed 1 July 2013).

Haiti Education Cluster (2010), *Survey on School Enrollment of the Children in Camps in Haiti*, 2010. Port-au-Prince: Haiti Education Cluster.

—— (2011), *Etat des Lieux des Ecoles – Un An Après le Séisme*, Port-au-Prince: Haiti Education Cluster.

—— (2012), *The Education Cluster in Haiti – Two Year On*, Available at: http://haiti-now.org/wp-content/uploads/2012/08/122011-Two_Year_On_Haiti_Education_Cluster_Unicef.pdf (accessed 1 July 2013).

Inter-Agency Network for Education in Emergencies (INEE) (2010), *INEE Minimum Standards for Education in Emergencies*, Available at: http://www.ineesite.org/en/minimum-standards (accessed 1 July 2013).

Inter-Agency Standing Committee (IASC) (2006), Guidance Note on Using the Cluster Approach to Strengthen Humanitarian Response, Available at: http://clusters.humanitarianresponse.info/document/iasc-guidance-note-using-cluster-approach-strengthen-humanitarian-response (accessed 1 July 2013).

Ministère de l'Education Nationale et la Formation Professionnelle (MENFP) (2010), *Plan Operationnel 2010–2015*, Available at: http://planipolis.iiep.unesco.org/upload/Haiti/Haiti_Plan_operationnel_2010-2015.pdf (accessed 1 July 2013).

—— (2012a), *Recensement Scolaire 2010–2011*, Port-au-Prince: MENFP.

—— (2012b), *Programme de la Scolarisation Universelle Gratuite et Obligatoire (PSUGO) (2012): Rapport sur l'Etat des lieux couvrant la période d'Octobre2011 à juin 2012*, Port-au-Prince: MENFP.

—— (2012c), Rapport de Synthèse de l'Atelier de Réflexion sur la Situation des Enfants Non- Scolarisés et des Elèves Surâgés du Système Educatif Haïtien, Port-au-Prince: MENFP.

Ministère de la Santé Publique et de la Population (MSPP) (2006), Enquête de Mortalité, Morbiditéet Utilisation des Services (EMMUS) IV, Available at: http://www.measuredhs.com/pubs/pdf/FR192/FR192.pdf (accessed 1 July 2013).

—— (2012), *Enquête de Mortalité, Morbidité et Utilisation des Services (EMMUS) V*, Available at: http://www.mspp.gouv.ht/site/downloads/Rapport%20preliminaire%20final%20EMMUS-V.pdf. (accessed 1 July 2013).

UNICEF (2010), Core Commitment for Children in Humanitarian Action, New York: UNICEF.

UNICEF and the UNESCO Institute for Statistics (2009), *Global Initiative on Out-of-School Children*, Available at: http://www.unicef.org/publications/files/CCC_042010.pdf (accessed 1 July 2013).

United Nations Development Programme (UNDP) (2007), *National Human Development Report for Haiti*, New York: UNDP.

Education, Hunger and Malnutrition in the Indian Context

T. Sundararaman and Anupama Hazarika

5

Chapter Outline

Introduction

Globally, prevalence of hunger has declined since the 1990s, yet remains 'serious'. Over 870 million people are hungry, out of which 97 per cent reside in developing countries. Despite impressive economic growth in the past decade, India ranks among the most undernourished countries in the world. Currently, the country finds itself with high levels of malnutrition affecting all ages and gender. It is also ranked among the 16 'alarming' countries for Hunger and ranks 65th in the Global Hunger Index amongst a list of 79 countries (IFPRI 2012).

It is well known that nutrition has a profound effect on physical health, and that it impairs neurological and cognitive development in a growing child and impairs the immunological response. Cognitive impairment results in declining ability to learn newer skills and impedes the individual's ability to lead a more productive life (WHO 2013). Malnutrition also leads to increased susceptibility to recurrent infections such as pneumonia, diarrhoeal diseases and tuberculosis among others, resulting in increased mortality especially in children below five years of age (WHO 2006). There is also a strong association between early nutritional deprivation and poor growth, delayed mental and cognitive development and economic productivity (Grantham-McGregor et al. 2007; Victora et al. 2008).

To add to this issue, poverty has intense effects through its numerous dimensions of inadequate food availability and depleting household food resources, resulting in poorer health, lack of adequate nutrition and deficient child care, and essentially deprives children from capabilities to survive, grow and reach their cognitive potential (MDG 2012; Boyle et al. 2006; Walker et al. 2007; Alderman 2007).

The reduction of child malnutrition has been recognized as one of the pillars for economic growth and development of the nation, and its importance is also reflected in the Millennium Development Goals (MDG) related to extreme poverty and hunger, and child survival. Given the effect of early childhood nutrition on physical health as well as cognitive development, improving nutrition also impacts MDG goals related to universal primary education, promotion of gender equality and empowerment of women, improvement of maternal health and combating diseases (MDG 2012).

This chapter addresses the issues faced in India, the policies to address them and the challenges therein, with an emphasis on the role of education.

Background

The rural poor, urban poor and victims of catastrophes have been recognized as the most at risk of hunger (FAO 2013). It is known that although the rural poor cultivate crops, catch fish or raise animals, they usually work as hired hands and do not own any land. This kind of work is often seasonal and it is difficult to set anything aside for emergencies. To add to their woes, the public health, education and sanitation services are of low quality and they lack basic amenities such as safe drinking water, making them more susceptible to diseases.

With the growth of urban areas and declining resources, there has been a constant migration of the poor to these areas. This population usually reside in deficient and unhygienic slums, devoid of the basic public health amenities and with very little means or resources to support themselves or their families. These people are at a constant risk of hunger, making them one of the most food-insecure populations. Additionally, armed conflicts and natural calamities such as floods, drought, hurricanes and earthquakes have led to victims of catastrophes to be also one of the most food-insecure and hungry populations (FAO 2013).

To combat hunger and food insecurity, the 1996 World Food Summit committed to cutting by half the number of undernourished people in the world by no later than 2015. One of the goals of the MDG also calls for a reduction by half of the proportion of people suffering from hunger between 1990 and 2015 (FAO 2013; MDG 2012).

Prevalence of hunger

During 2010–2012, it was estimated that 12.5 per cent of the global population or 870 million people were undernourished. Out of this, 852 million people reside in developing countries where prevalence of malnutrition is estimated to be 14.9 per cent. This prevalence of undernourishment has fallen from 23.2 per cent to 14.9 per cent during the period 1990–2010, while the incidence of poverty has declined from 47.5 per cent to 22.4 per cent and child mortality from 9.5 to 6.1 per cent. (IFPRI 2012).

The Global Hunger Index (GHI) for India has stagnated over the past decade. This is despite the fact that India's gross national income (GNI) during this period grew from 1460 US dollars (USD) to 2850 US dollars (USD). In 2008, the Indian State Hunger Index was calculated based on three variables, each of which were given equal weightage (Menon et al. 2008):

- The proportion of population that does not consume an adequate level of calories;
- The proportion of underweight children under five years of age; and,
- The mortality rate among children under five years of age, expressed as the percentage of children born alive who die before they reach the age of five.

This data revealed that over 230 million people in the country are 'food insecure' and suffer from chronic malnutrition (Bonnerjee and Koehler 2010). Thus, India's poor carry one-third to one-fourth of the global burden of food insecurity. In 11 states the hunger prevalence is alarming, while in Madhya Pradesh it is extremely alarming (Menon et al. 2008; Bonnerjee and Koehler 2010).

If the Indian states are compared with the GHI of nations for hunger prevalence, then the best performing state of Punjab lies below 33 developing countries and the worst performing states such as Bihar and Jharkhand rank closer to precariously positioned countries such as Zimbabwe and Haiti, and Madhya Pradesh between Ethiopia and Chad. Currently, even the states which have fared well economically have 'seriously high' levels of hunger (IFPRI 2012). A great limitation that is noted is that the Indian State Hunger Index was not repeated after 2008, due to want of national data such as the National Family Health Survey (NFHS) for the indicators (Figure 5.1).

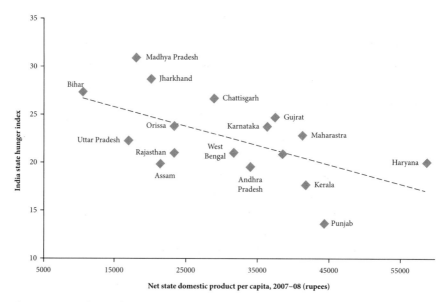

Figure 5.1 Correlation of India State Hunger Index with Net State Domestic Product per Capita

Source: Menon (2008)

Malnutrition in India

India experiences one of the highest levels of malnutrition in the world. Indeed, despite a very impressive economic growth for almost 15 years now, there is little progress in the reduction of malnutrition levels (Haddad 2009). The NHFS–3 data reveal that nearly one in every two children is malnourished. The alarming fact is that wasting, which reflects acute malnutrition, is nearly 20 per cent. Stunting, which reflects chronic malnutrition, has decreased, but is still as high as 48 per cent of the total under three-year population. Anaemia is prevalent in nearly 80 per cent of the children (IIPS 2007).

The Indian society has been traditionally stratified according to occupation, hierarchy and status accorded by society on religious grounds. For generations, stratification by status has remained static according to bloodlines, in what is known as the caste system. The people belonging to the lowest strata of this caste system have been ostracized, socially marginalized and deprived from fundamental rights for centuries. After independence, to bring justice and equality, under the Indian Constitution, these groups were classified into Schedule Castes (SC) and Schedule Tribes (ST). Other groups of the society which also remained on the fringes of the society were categorized as Other Backward Classes (OBC) (Sadangi 2008; Jaffrelot 2006). Affirmative action in terms of efforts to direct greater benefits and support to these sections of society was part of the state policy. Despite these policy directions, the evidence is that children belonging to these castes and tribes or other backward classes had relatively high levels of malnutrition by all three measures. Children belonging to the STs had the poorest nutritional status on almost every measure with very high prevalence of wasting. These figures are further aggravated due to sharp socio-economic, gender and cultural disparities. Thus, rural underweight prevalence is nearly 40 per cent higher than urban underweight (IIPS 2007).

More than half of the deaths amongst children have malnutrition as an underlying factor (WHO 2006). Most of these deaths are due to chronic hunger debilitating the individual so that one is prey to common diseases such as diarrhoea, pneumonia, measles, and tuberculosis, accounting for a greater part of these malnutrition-related deaths. Referring to Table 5.1, the NFHS–3 data when compared with the latest Sample Registration System (SRS) data (2012) reveal that infant mortality rates are higher in Indian states where malnutrition is more rampant. These include the states of Uttar

Table 5.1 Distribution of stunting, malnutrition and infant mortality rates in major Indian states

States	Height for age (Stunting)	Weight for age (malnutrition)	Infant mortality rate (IMR)
	Percentage below −3 SD	Percentage below − 3 SD	(SRS 2012)
INDIA	23.7	15.8	**44**
Andhra Pradesh	18.7	9.9	43
Arunachal Pradesh	21.7	11.1	32
Assam	20.9	11.4	55
Bihar	29.1	24.1	44
Chhattisgarh	24.8	16.4	48
Goa	10.2	6.7	11
Gujarat	25.5	16.3	41
Haryana	19.4	14.2	44
Himachal Pradesh	16	11.4	38
Jammu & Kashmir	14.9	8.2	41
Jharkhand	26.8	26.1	39
Karnataka	20.5	12.8	35
Kerala	6.5	4.7	12
Madhya Pradesh	26.3	27.3	59
Maharashtra	19.1	11.9	25
Manipur	13.1	4.7	11
Meghalaya	29.8	27.7	52
Mizoram	17.7	5.4	34
Nagaland	19.3	7.1	21
NCT of Delhi	20.4	8.7	28
Orissa	19.6	13.4	57
Punjab	17.3	8	30
Rajasthan	22.7	15.3	52
Sikkim	17.9	4.9	26
Tamilnadu	10.9	6.4	22
Tripura	14.7	15.7	29
Uttar Pradesh	32.4	16.4	57
Uttarakhand	23.1	15.7	36
West Bengal	17.8	11.1	32

Source: IIPS 2007; SRS 2012.

Pradesh, Madhya Pradesh, Assam, Rajasthan, Chhattisgarh and Meghalaya (IIPS 2007; SRS 2012). Malnutrition in India is prevalent in every age group. With regard to adult nutrition, the NFHS–3 data also reveal that nearly 35 per cent of the Indian adults are underweight with a body mass index (BMI) of less than 18.5. The fact that these numbers have not decreased over the past ten years despite the economic growth is even more alarming (refer to

Table 5.2). Women are especially vulnerable, and in the 15 to 49 age group as much as 35.6 per cent of women are underweight (IIPS 2007).

Table 5.2 Status of malnutrition in India

Indicators	NFHS–2 (1998–1999) In percentage	NFHS–3 (2005–2006) In percentage
Stunting in children under 3 years of age	45.50	38.40
Wasting in children under 3 years of age	15.50	19.10
Under weight in children under 3 years of age	47.0	45.9
Women aged 15–24 with BMI <18.5		44.1
Women aged 25–49 with BMI <18.5		30.7
Women aged 15–49 with BMI <18.5	36.2	35.6
Men aged 15–24 with BMI <18.5		47.3
Men aged 25–49 with BMI <18.5		26.9
Men aged 15–49 with BMI <18.5	NA	34.2

Source: IIPS 2007

Malnutrition in women affects the population in many ways. In pregnancy, malnutrition is associated with low birth weight of babies, more complications in pregnancy and at child birth, anaemia, more frequent abortions and higher maternal mortality. Intergenerational effects of poverty and malnutrition are also evident through various studies. Martorell and Zongrone (2012) documented that low birth weight, child stunting and delivery complications were correlated with intergenerational effects of maternal poverty and malnutrition.

They note that there are also socio-cultural factors at play, such as the fear of giving birth to a large baby, which leads to 'eating down' during pregnancy (Martorell and Zongrone 2012; Currie and Morretti 2005). Maternal nutrition has a profound effect on foetal growth and may be a marker for future chronic diseases such as diabetes mellitus and cardiovascular diseases. Cognitive development and school performance is one area where there is a direct link with malnutrition. Stunted children learn less than normal children and learn it slower (WHO 2006; Grantham-McGregor et al. 2007).

Economic productivity is also linked to malnutrition. Currie and Morretti (2005) examined long-term effects of maternal low birth weight. They found that low birth weight has significant effects on socio-economic outcomes in later life. Additionally, Johnson and Schoeni (2007) maintain that low birth weight is strongly related to poorer adult health and lowers adult annual earnings by 17.5 per cent. There is also evidence that *every year of schooling increases adult yearly income by 9%. The loss of adult income for being stunted but not in poverty is 22.2%, the loss from living in poverty but not being stunted is 5.9% and from being both stunted and in poverty is 19.8%. Clearly, when large number of children are affected, national development will also be substantially affected.* (Grantham-McGregor et al. 2007, p. 67)

Interestingly, the NFHS–3 data also reveal that children of underweight mothers are 34 per cent more likely to be underweight and that children of mothers with little or no education are 66 per cent more likely to be underweight when compared with mothers having five years or more of education. Adolescent nutritional requirement as well becomes a pertinent point for discussion. Adolescence is a period of rapid growth and there is additional need for nutrients as well as energy. The NFHS–3 data also reveals that malnutrition rates are slightly more in adolescent males, the only period in the life cycle when it is so (IIPS 2007). Can this be attributed to differing levels of activity keeping in view India's cultural context? For young women, adolescence is the foundation to developing a healthy adulthood. Micronutrients are essential for skeletal growth and good nutrition will meet the requirement of future pregnancy and breast feeding (Story and Stang 2005). Thus, all evidence suggests that malnutrition at this stage not only leads to stunting but also compounds the risks associated with future pregnancies.

Factors affecting hunger and malnutrition and the contribution of education towards alleviating them

Poverty and the role of economic disparities

Poverty leads to malnutrition and food insecurity. Undernourishment has severe permanent consequences for physical and intellectual development, which helps entrench poverty. Thus hunger and poverty can become entwined in a vicious cycle and levels and trends in these indicators tend to be similar (Haddad 2009). It is now unquestionable that there has been a decline in per capita calorie consumption in India in the past few decades. Estimated monthly per capita cereal consumption fell from 13.4 to 11.35 kg (Government of India 2011).

The paradox in the Indian situation is that malnutrition has been rising in a period of high growth. For instance, India's real per capita income has increased from being two-thirds of Kenya's real per capita income in 1950 to two and a half times of Kenya's at present (Deaton and Dreze 2009). But at the same time, the percentage of underweight children in India is 43.5 per cent versus 16.5 per cent in Kenya, while stunting is 35.8 per cent for Kenya versus 47.9 per cent for India (WHO 2009). Thus, the high growth rate is not reflected in a corresponding improvement of nutrition levels.

One explanation for this is inequitable growth. Despite the overall growth in the national gross domestic product (GDP) in the past few decades, the corresponding evidence on decrease in poverty is highly disputed. The period from the 1990s has been marked by highly inequitable growth and deterioration in poverty reduction (Sen 2004; Patnaik 2007; 2013). The Planning Commission (2012) has a mechanism of classification based on income and calorie consumption of the individuals within the population. This yardstick is known as the Poverty Line. All individuals who earn less than Rupees 26 (0.44 US dollars) and receive less than 2,200 calories per day in rural areas, and Rupees 32 (0.54 US Dollars) and less than 2,100 calories per day in urban areas are termed as 'Below the Poverty Line' (BPL).

Based on this poverty line, the all-India Head Count Ratio (HCR) has declined by 7.3 per cent, from 37.2 per cent in the year 2004–2005 to 29.8 per cent in the year 2009–2010. Rural poverty accordingly has declined by 8 per cent from 41.8 per cent to 33.8 per cent and urban poverty by 4.8 per cent from 25.7 per cent to 20.9 per cent during the same period. In 2009–2010, state poverty ratios reveal the greatest decline in Himachal Pradesh, Madhya Pradesh, Maharashtra, Orissa, Sikkim, Tamil Nadu, Karnataka and Uttarakhand, of 10 per cent or more, while there has been an increase in the states of Assam, Meghalaya, Manipur, Mizoram and Nagaland. Some of the bigger states such as Bihar, Chhattisgarh and Uttar Pradesh have shown only marginal decline in the poverty ratio, particularly in rural areas (Planning Commission Press Release 2012).

Among the group, 47.4 per cent of STs are below the poverty line, followed by 42.3 per cent SCs and 31.9 per cent OBCs in rural India, against 33.8 per cent for all classes. In urban India, 34.1 per cent SCs, 30 per cent STs and 24.3 per cent OBCs exhibit poverty against 20.9 per cent for all classes. In rural areas, households with the education of 'primary level and lower' have the highest poverty ratio. In the states of Bihar and Chhattisgarh, nearly two-thirds of households with 'primary level of education or lower' are poor followed by 46.8 per cent in Uttar Pradesh and 47.5 per cent in Orissa. These trends are similar in urban settings. If one accounts for occupation, nearly 50 per cent of the rural poor are daily wage agricultural labourers, while 47.1 per cent of the urban poor work as casual labourers (Planning Commission Press Release 2012).

A ration card known as a BPL card is given to these vulnerable populations, so that they can buy food at lesser rates than those above the poverty line. Yet controversial methods were used to identify this poverty line, and were subject to tremendous scrutiny and received considerable criticism (Patnaik 2013). Critics felt that defining the poor in terms of the formal BPL card is to miss the larger part of the needy population that may be just above the BPL line. Thus, the BPL card currently remains an imperfect way to identify those in real need of food and assistance, especially sections of the population vulnerable to malnutrition. Pregnant women and young children form the largest group within this. Others that need to be reached include marginalized populations such as displaced tribals, fragmented families left behind by migration and disabled people, among others.

Poor access to health care, poor quality of health care and low levels of education (especially women's education) evidently have all contributed to the high levels of malnutrition and these closely relate to poverty. Based on the GHI, we note that between 1990 and 1996, India's GHI score was falling commensurate with economic growth. After 1996, however, this disparity between economic development and progress in the fight against hunger widened, with a small increase during 1996 and 2001 and after which there has been stagnation. If we compare this with the GHI scores of Sri Lanka, a country within the same region, it is evidenced that Sri Lanka has achieved impressively high literacy and life expectancy through welfare-oriented policies, investment in public health care and education systems, and a commitment to gender equality. Bangladesh, another neighbouring country, also shows a similar pattern benefitting from relatively broad-based social progress and more effective sector and public services that helped reduce child malnutrition among the poorest. Bangladesh has also closed the gender gap in education, and has overtaken India on a range of social indicators, including the level and rate of reduction of child mortality (IFPRI 2012). While China, a country with similar population patterns, has lower GHI scores than predicted from its level of economic development, through a strong commitment to poverty reduction, nutrition and health interventions and improved access to safe water, sanitation and education (IFPRI 2012).

Though poverty is one of the major determinants of malnutrition, it is worth considering why India's malnutrition levels are out of proportion to its level of poverty. India ranks second to last on child underweight out of 129 countries – below Ethiopia, Niger, Nepal and Bangladesh. Only Timor-Leste had a higher rate of underweight children. By comparison, only 23 per cent of children are underweight in sub-Saharan Africa (IFPRI 2012).

Education, through its multipronged approach, can contribute towards effective response to poverty by facilitating greater resources. This is mainly because it is more likely that an educated individual will secure a better job and work in safer and more consistent work environments. Better pay in stable jobs leads to increased access to more household resources, including food security.

Dietary factors and feeding practices

Poor feeding continues to affect a high proportion of children in developing countries. In India, most breast feeding and weaning practices are generally not appropriate. Nearly 62 per cent children do not receive colostrum, in up to 55.8 per cent infants weaning for semisolids is delayed, with just over half the children receiving complementary foods. It is found that infant weaning foods lack in energy-protein and micronutrients (Agarwal 2011). Our experience in the country reveals that due to associated cultural factors, there is a relative lack of access to non-milk animal proteins, which is a major difference from most nations. Animal food sources have not only higher, better absorbed protein, but also higher fats and protective elements. Diversity in terms of greens is also less (UNICEF 2008).

These issues of dietary diversity and choice of foods and feeding practices are not independent of poverty. The poor family has to optimize its limited food resources across so many mouths to feed, and unless supported by good nutrition counselling, the choices could be sub-optimal. The public food supplementation programmes also do not bring focus on diversity of food required to address child malnutrition. Currently, supplementation programmes provide largely cereal-based supplements, which are largely sub-optimal (Government of India 2011). Improved breast-feeding practices are estimated to save up to 1 million lives. Complementary feeding while breast feeding for up to two years or beyond could save up to half million lives by reducing the risk of infection leading to improved physical growth and motor development (UNICEF 2005; 2008).

Gender

A greater gender disparity is often cited as the reason that explains higher malnutrition levels in the South Asian context. Women's low status in India contributes to children's poor nutritional outcomes in the region because children's development and mothers' well-being are closely linked: women's poor nutritional status, low education and low social status undermine their ability to give birth to well-nourished babies and to adequately feed and care for their children. Gender disparity also acts through the burden of work on the mother, leaving little time for child care, in which she has a disproportionately high share. Gender disparity could effect maternal malnutrition and poor access to health care for women. Several studies in rural Nepal, Peru, India and Indonesia have suggested that malnutrition can result from inequities in food distribution and preferential child care practices that favour certain age and sex groups within societies even when food supplies are sufficient. The relationship between child gender and nutrition may be moderated by a variety of factors including cultural values, birth order or sex ratio of children in the family and household decisions on allocation of supplementary food resources (Walker et al. 2007; Escobal 2005; Ranis et al. 2000; Gittelsohn et al. 1997; Graham 1997, Pande 2003; Ralston 1997; Van Esterik 1984; Pelto 1987).

Underutilization of health care services

Studies indicate that one of the key factors for poor nutritional status of children especially in urban slums of India is underutilization of maternal health services. Poor illiterate mothers additionally have poorer access to good dietary and hygiene practices leading to adverse pregnancy outcomes, low birth weight of the infant and poor nutritional status of the child. Additionally, there is also the likelihood of dropouts from scheduled vaccination, leading to more susceptibility to recurrent infections, and consequently malnutrition. The low utilization of health services may be due to high out-of-pocket expenditures to access health services and transportation, and low awareness of health-promoting behaviours. Additionally, it is also found that in these resource-constraint settings in India there are shortages of human resources for health, poor infrastructure, overcrowding and weak referral systems. Lack of motivation of the health care providers and poor communication with the patients create further hurdles and negatively impact the child's health (Kumar and Singh 2013; Singh et al. 2003; Wagstaff 2004).

Policies and programmes in India to address the issues of hunger and malnutrition

In 1993, the government implemented the National Nutrition Policy (NNP). The NNP recognized hunger and malnutrition as a multidimensional problem. It advocated a comprehensive inter-sectoral strategy to address the multipronged issues of malnutrition. The NPP initiated direct nutritional interventions for the vulnerable 'at-risk' populations as well as various direct and indirect institutional and structural changes.

The direct interventions included expanding the safety net for nutrition interventions, especially for vulnerable groups including mother and child; initiating appropriate behavioural changes in adolescents, especially those living in urban slums; fortification of essential foods with micronutrients such as iodine, iron and folic acid; and popularization of low-cost nutritious foods, among others.

The indirect structural changes sought to address issues with food security by distributing food grains, improving the dietary pattern through production and demonstration, initiating land reforms, addressing health and basic nutrition through education and prevention of food adulteration. It also sought to address issues of minimum wage, equal remuneration for men and women and special emphasis to improve employment opportunities for women.

Over the years, the Indian government has also implemented very unique and large food security and nutrition-related programmes. These can be broadly classified as follows, with a few examples for each:

1. **Nutrition-related schemes:** The Integrated Child Development Services (ICDS) scheme and the mid-day meal scheme (MDM) in primary schools;
2. **Food security programmes:** Public Distribution Scheme (PDS) in Antyodaya, Annapurna Yojana;
3. **Livelihood-related programmes:** The National Rural Employment Guarantee Act (NREGA), the Sampoorna Grameen Rozgar Yojana (SGRY), National Food for Work Programme and the Rashtriya Sam Vikas Yojana (RSVY);
4. **Health and social security programmes:** National Rural Health Mission, Integrated Child Development Scheme (ICDS), National Maternity Benefit Scheme (NMBS), National Old Age Pension Scheme (NOAPS), National Family Benefit Scheme (NFBC); and
5. **Drinking water and sanitation-related schemes:** Accelerated Rural Water Supply Programme (ARWSP), Swajaldhara and the Central Rural Sanitation Programme (CRSP).

The actual investment in and implementation of these programmes, however, fall short of what is required. There is poor coordination across programmes and there is a lack of accountability at multiple levels. The ability of the citizen to enforce their rights and secure their entitlements is limited – especially in the context of hunger (Save the Children 2009).

It is in this context that we examine the potential of education to act as an empowering force, liberating the poor household from hunger, malnutrition and poverty.

Education as a response to hunger and malnutrition

While there are many inputs required to address hunger and malnutrition, one of the inputs that would require relatively less economic and political changes and therefore easier to negotiate is a greater investment in education.

We note from Figure 5.2 a positive correlation of female literacy with decline in malnutrition as well as infant mortality (refer to Figure 5.3). Though all states have high levels of hunger, it is noted that most states with better female literacy rates, such as Kerala and Mizoram, have better scores for malnutrition and infant mortality for children, while states like Madhya Pradesh, Jharkhand, Bihar, Rajasthan, Uttar Pradesh and Chhattisgarh, which have illiteracy more than the national average, fare worse in parameters of hunger, malnutrition and child mortality.

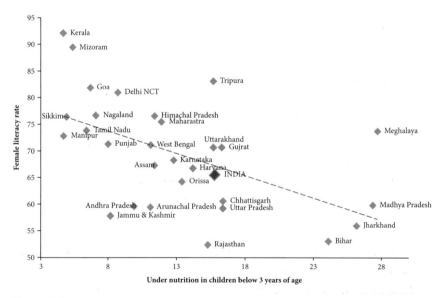

Figure 5.2 Correlation of female literacy rates with child malnutrition in Indian states

Source: Census of India, 2011

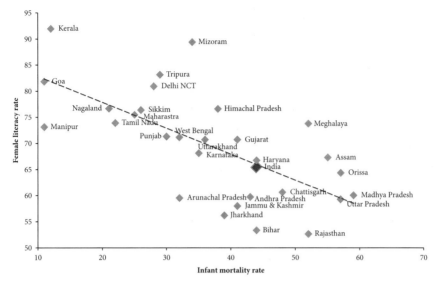

Figure 5.3 Correlation of state-wise female literacy with infant mortality rates

Source: Census of India, 2011

Since the early 1980s, there has been a resurgence of interest in the role of the mother or caregiver on child's growth. Relevant maternal characteristics include her education, mental health and self-confidence, intelligence, knowledge and beliefs, autonomy and control of resources, reasonable workload and availability of time and family and community social support. Of these, the most amenable to social action is the education of women. Relying on the strong correlation between maternal education and child health, public policy discourse has increasingly argued for investment in women's education, both as an end in itself and as the most effective means for achieving a wide number of social goals – ranging from better sanitation practices to smaller family size, from lowered child mortality to enhanced child nutrition and child survival (Batty et al. 2009; Black et al 2008; Pelto 1987).

A number of studies have shown that children of educated mothers experience lower co-morbidities such as gastrointestinal disorders, inadequate nutritional status and lower mortality and achieve better health outcomes and higher growth than children of uneducated mothers. While mother's education was found to have a positive effect on long-term nutritional status, as measured by stunting, evidence also suggests this is more important in the earlier years of child growth.

Studies in developing countries indicate that higher levels of maternal education are related to increased knowledge and understanding of health information and use of health services (Escobal 2005; Wachs 2008). Utilization of health-promoting activities such as vaccination and vitamin A supplementation for their children is more likely when the mother is educated and this in turn positively influences her child's physical growth. A longitudinal study in Bangladesh suggests that improved feeding practices and cleanliness positively correlate to maternal education. Mothers were likely to feed the child more frequently, with fresh food and in a cleaner, more protected environment. Education may also affect health through a reduction in the number of pregnancies and the number of children, which allows more resources to be devoted to the surviving children (Semba et al. 2008; Guldan et al. 1993).

Evidence also suggests that associations between mothers' level of education and the physical growth of their children involves her greater participation in important family decisions, as mothers are more likely than fathers to allocate family resources in ways that promote their child's nutrition. There is also evidence that mothers in low family resource settings make more appropriate decisions on resource allocation when the mothers have increased levels of schooling. Knowledge and verbal skill enhance mothers' ability to be successful in decision-making situations, and empower them through access to outside resources like job opportunities (Desai 2000; Wach 2008).

Maternal education may thus transmit information about health and nutrition directly, by enabling mothers to acquire information, and exposing them to new environments, thus making them receptive to modern medical treatments. It imparts self-confidence which enhances the woman's role in intra-household decision making. The self-confidence generated through education enables her to interact better with health professionals, helping her to make informed choices (Glewwe 1999).

In recent years researchers have begun to acknowledge the influence of fathers on the development of their young children. Fathers assume multiple roles in families, which influences children in numerous ways, directly and indirectly. A study in Pakistan revealed a higher contribution towards household resources by educated fathers (Aslam and Kingdon 2010). It was also noted that most of the uneducated or poorly educated fathers worked in informal sectors where the work is often irregular and the income low, leading to lower economic status which often resulted in improper dietary practices, underutilization of health care services, and poor living conditions that are detrimental to child health (Miller and Rodgers 2009).

Paternal education along with maternal education is a strong predictor of child growth, as evidenced by these studies. The education of parents is often used as an indicator of the quality of time children spend with their parents. It has been hypothesized that better-educated parents are more concerned and involved with their children's development as they are aware of children's developmental needs (McBride and Mills 1993; Bailey 1993; Yeung et al. 2001; Blair et al. 1994).

The findings of a recent IFPRI study imply that in the absence of concurrent improvements in health and education, only modest impacts on child malnutrition in India are to be expected from income growth. A multisectoral, well-coordinated approach is needed to successfully fight child malnutrition in India and elsewhere (Von Braun et al. 2008; Headey et al. 2012).

India has moved on a number of fronts to improve food security and nutrition in past years and has recognized the need for multisectoral action. The government operates several large-scale, nutrition-relevant social programmes, but poor design, low coverage and insufficient monitoring are continual challenges. In the absence of up-to-date information on nutrition outcomes, programme effectiveness remains uncertain. Home to the majority of the world's undernourished children, India is in dire need of monitoring systems for child malnutrition and related indicators that produce data at regular intervals, in order to improve programme performance and scale up impact (IFPRI 2012).

Conclusion

Hunger and malnutrition presents a persistent challenge in India, despite the impressive economic growth. It is our contention that the main determinant of this is poverty. But poverty acts in many ways. It acts through decreased ability to purchase food of sufficient quantity, quality and diversity. Poverty acts through less time for effective child care. Poverty acts through less access to education. Poverty acts through less access to public services. A vicious cycle is created between poverty and hunger, where chronic hunger leads to lower cognitive development, which in-turn exacerbates poverty. Also, malnutrition leads to severe and frequent infection which in turn increases malnutrition.

And children with recurrent infections and malnutrition have lesser cognitive development, even when in school.

Governments can, therefore, for the same level of economic development achieve much better reductions in hunger, malnutrition and poverty and much better improvements in health through effective public services that intervene and disrupt these vicious cycles. Of all these interventions that the government can make, perhaps the most important is education, for it is the most empowering.

Education provides the poor household, especially the women, with the knowledge, skills and confidence required to make optimal choices with their available resources on food. Education is critical to better awareness of entitlements and being able to negotiate better access to these entitlements. It allows for greater access to employment opportunities and higher levels of income. Above all, education enables and empowers them to reflect on their own condition and aspire to change it.

Questions for reflection

1. Higher levels of parental education have been associated with lower levels of malnutrition and illness. What could be the pathways through which education has this positive effect?
2. How do health and education contribute to economic growth?
3. Does economic growth always lead to lower levels of hunger and malnutrition? What are the circumstances under which this happens or fails to happen?

Further reading

1. Drèze, J. and Sen, A. (1991). *Hunger and Public Action*. Oxford: Oxford University Press

    The role of public action in solving hunger has been studied in this book. It interprets concepts of entitlements and capabilities, while exploring the interaction of nutritional, economic, social and political elements and their influence on hunger and deprivation.

2. Govinda, R. and Diwan, R. (eds) (2003). *Community Participation and Empowerment in Primary Education*. New Delhi: Sage Publications.

    This book presents the grassroots experiences, problems encountered and lessons learnt from initiatives launched in five Indian states, namely Madhya Pradesh, Karnataka, Rajasthan, Bihar and Kerala. The contributors cover a range of important issues, among others, the equitable distribution of participation, and ensuring the genuine representation of those who are traditionally excluded from decision making in rural areas.

3. Herz, B. and Sperling, G. (2004). *What Works in Girls' Education: Evidence and Policies from the Developing World*. New York: Council of Foreign Relations Press.

This report packages an extensive body of research on the state of girls' education and the impact thereof on families, economies and educational quality. It argues that investing in girls' education globally delivers huge returns for economic growth, political participation, women's health, smaller and more sustainable families and disease prevention.

References

Agarwal, K. N. (2011). Weaning practices in other parts of the world: case study India. In K. N. Agarwal, H. van Goudoever, S. Guandalini, and R. E. Kleinman (Eds). *Early Nutrition: Impact on Short- and Long-Term Health*. Nestlé Nutr Inst Workshop Ser Pediatr Program. Nestec Ltd. Vevey/S. Karger AG Basel, 2011, vol 68, pp. 107–115 (DOI: 10.1159/000325670).

Alderman, H. (2007). Improving nutrition through community growth promotion: longitudinal study of the nutrition and early child development program in Uganda. *World Development*, *35*(8), 1376–1389.

Aslam, M. and Kingdon, G. (2010). *Parental Education and Child Health: Understanding the Pathways of Impact in Pakistan*. Centre for the Study of African Economies Working Paper Series/2010–2016.

Bailey, W. T. (1993). Fathers' knowledge of development and involvement with preschool children. *Perceptual and Motor Skills*, *77*(3), 1032–1034.

Batty, G. D., Shipley, M. J., Gunnell, D., Huxley, R., Kivimaki, M., Woodward, M. and Smith, G. D. (2009). Height, wealth, and health: an overview with new data from three longitudinal studies. *Economics & Human Biology*, *7*(2), 137–152.

Black, R. E., Allen, L. H., Bhutta, Z. A., Caulfield, L. E., De Onis, M., Ezzati, M. and Rivera, J. (2008). Maternal and child undernutrition: global and regional exposures and health consequences. *The Lancet*, *371*(9608), 243–260.

Blair, S. L., Wenk, D. A. and Hardesty, C. (1994). Marital quality and paternal involvement interconnections of men's spousal and parental roles. *The Journal of Men's Studies* 2(3), 221–237.

Bonnerjee, A. and Koehler, G. (2010). *World Economy & Development. Hunger: The True Growth Story in India*, 2(3), 221–237.

Boyle, M. H., Racine, Y., Georgiades, K., Snelling, D., Hong, S., Omariba, W. et al. (2006). The influence of economic development level, household wealth and maternal education on child health in the developing world. *Social Science & Medicine*, *63*(8), 2242–2254.

Currie, J. and Moretti, E. (2005). Biology as destiny? Short and long-run determinants of intergenerational transmission of birth weight. NBER working paper no 11567 (JEL 11). 1–26.

Deaton, A. and Drèze, J. (2009). Food and nutrition in India: facts and interpretations. *Economic and Political Weekly*, *44*(7), 42–65.

Desai, S. (2000). Maternal education and child health: a feminist dilemma. *Feminist Studies 26*(2), 425–446.

Escobal, J., Saavedra, J., Suárez, P., Huttly, S., Penny, M., Lanata, C. et al. (2005). The interaction of public assets: private assets and community characteristics and its effect on early childhood height-for-age in Peru. *Young Lives Working Paper*, *14*.

Food and Agriculture Organizaton. *FAQs and Basic Definitions*. Available at http://www.fao.org/hunger/en/. (Accessed on 16 May 2013).

Gittelsohn, J., Thapa, M. and Landman, L. T. (1997). Cultural factors, caloric intake and micronutrient sufficiency in rural Nepali households. *Social Science & Medicine*, *44*(11), 1739–1749.

Glewwe, P. (1999). Why does mother's schooling raise child health in developing countries? Evidence from Morocco. *Journal of Human Resources*, *34*(1), 124–159.

Government of India. (2011). *Levels and Patterns of Consumer Expenditure (2009–2010)*. 538 (66/1.0/1). December 2011.

Graham, M. A. (1997). Food allocation in rural Peruvian households: concepts and behavior regarding children. *Social Science & Medicine*, *44*(11), 1697–1709.

Grantham-McGregor, S., Cheung, Y. B., Cueto, S., Glewwe, P., Richter, L. and Strupp, B. (2007). Developmental potential in the first 5 years for children in developing countries. *The Lancet*, *369*(9555), 60–70.

Guldan, G. S., Zeitlin, M. F., Beiser, A. S., Super, C. M., Gershoff, S. N. and Datta, S. (1993). Maternal education and child feeding practices in rural Bangladesh. *Social Science & Medicine*, *36*(7), 925–935.

Haddad, L. (2009). Lifting the curse: overcoming persistent undernutrition in India. *IDS Bulletin*, *40*(4), 1–8.

Headey, D., Chiu, A. and Kadiyala, S. (2012). Agriculture's role in the Indian enigma: help or hindrance to the crisis of undernutrition? *Food Security*, *4*(1), 87–102.

IFPRI. (2012). Global Hunger Index. *The Challenge of Hunger: Ensuring Sustainable Food Security Under Land, Water, And Energy Stresses*. Washington DC: IFPRI.

International Institute of Population Sciences (IIPS) and Macro International. (2007). *National Family Health Survey (NFHS 3), 2005–2006: India; Volume 1*. Mumbai: IIPS.

Jaffrelot, C. (2006). The impact of affirmative action in India: more political than socioeconomic. *India Review*, *5*(2), 173–189.

Johnson, R. C. and Schoeni, R. F. (2007). The influence of early-life events on human capital, health status, and labor market outcomes over the life course. *Journal of Economic Analysis & Policy*, *11*(3), 1–57.

Kumar, A. and Singh, A. (2013). Decomposing the gap in childhood undernutrition between poor and non-poor in Urban India, 2005–2006. *PloS One*, *8*(5), e64972.

Martorell, R. and Zongrone, A. (2012). Intergenerational influences on child growth and undernutrition. *Paediatric and Prenatal Epidemiology*, *26*(1), 302–314.

McBride, B. A. and Mills, G. (1993). A comparison of mother and father involvement with their preschool age children. *Early Childhood Research Quarterly*, *8*(4), 457–477.

Menon, P., Deolalikar, A. and Bhaskar, A. (2008). Comparisons of hunger across states: India state hunger index. *International Food Policy Research Institute*. 1–18. Riverside: University of California.

Millennium Development Goals. (2012). *The Millennium Development Goals Report*. New York: United Nations.

Miller, J. E. and Rodgers, Y. V. (2009). Mother's education and children's nutritional status: new evidence from Cambodia. *Asian Development Review*, *26*(1), 131–165.

Pande, R. P. (2003). Selective gender differences in childhood nutrition and immunization in rural India: the role of siblings. *Demography*, *40*(3), 395–418.

Patnaik P (2013a). *Poverty has increased during period of economic growth, says economist.* The Hindu. 20 May 2013.

——— (2013b). *A Critique of the Welfare-Theoretic Basis of the Measurement of Poverty.* Economic & Political Weekly, 48(14), 17.

——— (2007). Neoliberalism and rural poverty in India. *Economic and Political Weekly*, 3132–3150.

Pelto, G. H. (1987). Cultural issues in maternal and child health and nutrition. *Social Science & Medicine*, *25*(6), 553–559.

Planning Commission Press Release. (2012). Press note on poverty estimates, 2009–2010. Planning Commission, *Government of India* (press_pov1903. pdf).

Ralston, K. (1997). Children's health as an input to labor: intra household food distribution in rural Indonesia. *Journal of Policy Modeling*, *19*(5), 567–586.

Ranis, G., Stewart, F. and Ramirez, A. (2000). Economic growth and human development. *World Development*, *28*(2), 197–219.

Sadangi, H. C. (2008). *Emancipation of Dalits and Freedom Struggle.* New Delhi: Gyan Publishing House. *Vital Statistics Department*, *47*(2), 1–6.

Save the Children. (2009). Freedom from Hunger. An Outline For Save the Children and Civil Society Involvement in Child Undernutrition in India.

Sen, A. Himanshu (2004a):"*Poverty and Inequality in India*," Economic and Political Weekly, 39(38(1918)), 4247–4263.

——— (2004b). *Poverty and Inequality in India: II: Widening Disparities during the 1990s.* Economic and Political Weekly, 4361–4375.

Semba, R. D., de Pee, S., Sun, K., Sari, M., Akhter, N. and Bloem, M. W. (2008). Effect of parental formal education on risk of child stunting in Indonesia and Bangladesh: a cross-sectional study. *The Lancet*, *371*(9609), 322–328.

Singh, S., Jacqueline, E. D., Michael, V. and Jennifer, N. (2003). *Adding It Up: The Benefits of Investing in Sexual and Reproductive Health Care.* New York NY, Alan Guttmacher Institute/UNFPA.

Story, M. and Stang, J. (2005). *Nutrition Needs of Adolescents: Guidelines for Adolescent Nutrition Services.* Minneapolis: University of Minnesota, 21–34.

UNICEF. (2005). *State of World's Children.* New York: United Nations Children's Fund (UNICEF), 1–151.

———. (2008). *The State of the World's Children.* New York: United Nations Children's Fund (UNICEF), 1–154.

Van Esterik, P. (1984). *Intra-family Food Distribution: Its Relevance for Maternal and Child Nutrition.* Cornell University: Division of Nutritional Sciences, New York State Colleges of Human Ecology & Agriculture and Life Sciences.

Victora, C. G., Adair, L., Fall, C., Hallal, P. C., Martorell, R., Richter, L. and Sachdev, H. S. (2008). Maternal and child undernutrition: consequences for adult health and human capital. *Lancet*, *371*(9609), 340–357.

Von Braun, J., Ruel, M. and Gulati, A. (2008). Accelerating progress toward reducing child malnutrition in India: a concept for action (No. 12). *International Food Policy Research Institute* (IFPRI).

Wachs, T. D. (2008). Multiple influences on children's nutritional deficiencies: a systems perspective. *Physiology & Behavior, 94*(1), 48–60.

Wagstaff, A. (2004). *The Millennium Development Goals for Health: Rising to the Challenges*. Washington, DC: World Bank.

Walker, S. P., Wachs, T. D., Meeks Gardner, J., Lozoff, B., Wasserman, G. A., Pollitt, E. and Carter, J. A. (2007). Child development: risk factors for adverse outcomes in developing countries. *The Lancet, 369*(9556), 145–157.

World Health Organization. (2006). *WHO Child Growth Standards: Length/Height-for-Age, Weight-for-Age, Weight-for-Length, Weight-for-Height and Body Mass Index-for-age: Methods and Development*. World Health Organization 1–307.

—— (2009). *World Health Statistics 2009*. Geneva: World Health Organization.

——. (2013). *Malnutrition. Maternal, Newborn, Child and Adolescent Health*. Available at http://www.who.int/maternal_child_adolescent/topics/child/malnutrition/en/. Accessed on 17 May 2013.

Yeung, W. J., Sandberg, J. F., Davis-Kean, P. E., and Hofferth, S. L. (2001). Children's time with fathers in intact families. *Journal of Marriage and Family, 63*(1), 136–115.

Education and Poverty in the Philippines

Lorraine Pe Symaco

6

Chapter Outline

Introduction

The role of education in development has often been the basis for re-orientating policies which favour the increasing function of the education sector in poverty alleviation, as demonstrated especially in developing countries (Pham and Fry 2011; Noonan 2011; Ahrens and McNamara 2013; Symaco 2013). The prominent human capital theory emphasized long ago (Harbison and Myers 1964) the role of education in bringing about economic advancement and has been a major theoretical perspective in studies highlighting the role of mass expansion of education in development. Of course, critiques of the theory do exist, one of which points out the failure of the theory to take into account how the structure of such capital formation affects 'social relations and increasing disparities between different human groups or classes' (Symaco 2013). Despite this, the role of education in development has been echoed widely, as exemplified in global calls such as UNESCO's 'Education for All' and similarly the United Nations' 'Millennium Development Goals' with its Universal Primary Education (UPE) programme.

But what exactly is the role of education in development – particularly in the alleviation of poverty as desired more by, but not limited to, developing countries? How does poverty in turn affect the chances of people acquiring 'good education'? This chapter shall discuss the issues of education, poverty and malnourishment in the Philippines and matters relating to such. It will also look at the policies implemented by the government to combat the concerns of poverty and malnutrition, and the particular role of education in improving the social and economic welfare of the poor.

What is poverty?

With the virtually unquestioned link between educational achievement and poverty, and numerous studies dealing with the effects of poverty on general well-being, how do we define poverty? The multidimensional feature, which evades the prevalent unidimensional association of the term with low levels of income, is argued by van der Berg (2008) when he expounds on Sen's characterization of poverty as an effect of the absence of the 'capability to function effectively in society' (p. 1). Expounding further on this definition, the inability to access basic services such as education can be considered as 'poverty'. Similarly, Carr (2008) proposed the notion of 'poverties' with the idea of incorporating the multiple 'complex barriers to human well-being that emerge in particular places' (p. 727). Carr argues further that taking a universalistic account of poverty risks shapes the identification of the issue in three ways: (a) preconceived notions are relied upon in terms of accessing solutions for poverty alleviation, with foundation solutions (e.g. capitals) seen as *the* solution for the global concern; (b) if poverty is viewed as being the same everywhere, there runs the risk of the inability to examine further what poverty means to the actual poor, promoting the need to seek interventions that might not be relevant to the communities in question and; (c) as relevant to (b), treating poverty as a singular account we 'overlook potential gains and compromises ... because we cannot consider and plan for the new opportunities and challenges that will inevitably accompany any change in a local context' (pp. 727–728).

Assuming the multidimensional features of poverty as defined above, it should be acknowledged that poverty does affect other areas such as education, health and income, among others. It should also be noted that such sectors (i.e. education, health) are interdependent and 'compartmentalizing' solutions run the risk of actually realizing a solution for poverty alleviation.

Education, development and poverty

The rhetoric of education as being the 'great equalizer' that will bring people out of poverty is nothing short of familiar. Literature documents various studies highlighting the role of education in poverty alleviation (Mohd Asri 2012; Brock and Symaco 2011; van der Berg 2008), the link of family background and socio-economic status to educational outcomes (Raffo et al. 2009; Wikeley et al. 2008; UNICEF 2007), and generally the role of education in socio-economic development (Symaco 2011; Boughton 2013; Hayden and Le 2013), among others. And with the rise of globalization and internationalization of services, the idea of the knowledge-based society has never been as relevant as it is now. Particularly, studies (Symaco 2013b; 2012; Welch 2013) support the role of education (i.e. higher education) in equipping human capital with necessary skills to function effectively in this type of society and approaching the requisite state of advancement. However, the modernisms associated with the knowledge-based economy, like that of the information and communication technology (ICT), have aggravated the movement of poor communities farther beyond the periphery. Despite the overall advancement that can be seen in societies, and the connectivity through virtual worlds that ICT has introduced, greater divergence endures as a considerable number of individuals who lack essential and basic services (e.g. shelter, electricity) continue to exist.

Studies (Raffo et al. 2009; UNDP 1997) also point out the inability of poor communities to revel in the supposed benefits of education given their lack of opportunity to access such basic services. Bourdieu in his analysis of the 'cultural capital' recounts the disadvantage faced by individuals from the lower class level in gaining entry to educational institutions mainly because of their 'inherent lack of familiarity in their backgrounds', with the programme content of such institutions seemingly favouring the middle class (Symaco 2010, p. 265). Drop-out rates also remain high, especially in developing countries, where students often stop schooling due to lack of financial resources to continue or, relatedly, to help the family earn a living by working when their parents deem the children fit. While economic growth has been at the forefront of development policies, poverty alleviation, now more than ever, emerges as its fundamental objective (Carr 2008).

It is not surprising then that a number of studies from the past to the present are devoted to exploring the effects that education has specifically on poverty alleviation and their links, equally as paramount as the general 'education and development' discourse. For instance, Thurow (1967) long ago suggested that an overall improvement in the entire education section will result in poverty alleviation, while Bardhan (1996) has emphasized the significance of gender equity through better education for women which can, in turn, result in better education for their children (particularly their daughters). Bardhan also highlights how the lack of efficient services in poor communities, such as childcare centres, forces the daughters of young mothers to skip school in order to take care of their younger siblings, thus perpetuating the cycle of low education from one generation to the next (p. 1352). Education and health are considered important factors that can help break the intergenerational cycle of poverty. In addition, Wiekeley et al. (2008) explored the link between educational relationship and poverty. The study suggests that students in poor communities lack the proper support and children/adult relationships, leading to negative educational outcomes. The effect of conflict and poverty on low or nil educational opportunities is also documented in literature (Boughton, 2013; Symaco 2013).

It should be noted though that educational policy interventions relating to poverty alleviation are not exclusively confined to developing countries, as this book also shows. In literature, studies have shown various educational policy contraventions aimed at ending the link between poor educational outcomes and poverty incidence (Raffo et al. 2009; Melin 2001). The role of poverty in non-access to educational services and the distinct advantage of students coming from higher socio-economic status in terms of educational attainment and performance are also supported. Sen (as cited in Melin 2001) also links education and poverty alleviation 'directly, because of its relevance to the well-being and freedom of people, indirectly through influencing social change, and indirectly through influencing economic production' (p. 6).

Country context

The Philippines, located in South East Asia and home to close to 100 million people, ranks as the 12th most populous country in the world (UNFP 2012). With an expanding population, it is also one of the youngest in the region (second only to Laos), with a median age of 23.3 (CIA 2013). As a predominantly Catholic country and with the conservative Catholic Church's expanding influence in state affairs, the Philippines remains as the only nation in the world that prohibits divorce, and the controversial 'Reproductive Health' bill, which guarantees access to contraception and fertility control, among others, runs a risk in actual implementation. On the one hand, the poverty incidence among the population is at 27.9 per cent, which has remained virtually unchanged from the 28 per cent figure of 2006 and 2009. Poverty incidence remains highest in the conflict-ridden Autonomous Region of Muslim Mindanao (ARMM), estimated at 47 per cent (among families) compared to the rest of the country. The estimated cost of poverty eradication is almost 80 billion Philippines pesos (Php)[1] (for the first semester of 2012), while the actual budget for the Cash Conditional Transfer programme of the Department of Social Welfare and Development (DSWD) was 39 billion Php for the entire year of 2012 (NCSB 2013).

The connection among low (to nil) education, population and poverty is documented in literature, as in, for example, the study conducted by UNFP (2013), which indicates that the poorest and least educated women in rural areas in sub-Saharan Africa display the lowest rates of contraceptive use. In the Philippines, its large population is also linked to poverty, where poor communities are characterized mainly by large families (6 members or more) and with the head of the household having only attained the primary level of schooling (ADB 2009). There is also the observed move of communities from rural or provincial areas to Metropolitan Manila, with the city recording close to 12 million residents. While the poverty incidence among families is lowest in the National Capital Region (i.e. Metropolitan Manila and surrounding regions) at 3.8 per cent in 2012 (NCSB 2013), this 'push' factor (Iredale 2001) of residents from provincial areas to the city is evident in their desire to secure job placements which most people deem abundant in Manila. Naturally, given this massive influx of people, communities unable to secure proper jobs in the cities contribute to the continuous rise of the urban poor. In 2012, an Executive Order maintained the strengthening of the Presidential Commission for the Urban Poor (PCUP) and obligated the Commission to 'undertake social preparation activities related to ... human development and basic social service ... '.

Corruption in the Philippines

The calls to improve provision in terms of quality, greater access and equity are some of the focal concerns in education. Of course, as in any service, the need for transparency to achieve basic demands is essential. This brings to light the need for accountability and transparency in the provision of services in the education sector. Similar to any public sector service provider, education is as prone to corruption as others. The extent of corruption is said to reflect a country's economic, socio-political and cultural conditions (Hallak and Poisson 2002). Corruption is common to many developing countries, especially in their public sector systems, which are characterized by inefficiency. There is also a record of such malpractice in developed countries. Corruption in education varies in scale and form, from accepting bribes and academic plagiarism among faculty members and students to the absence of fair bidding for the printing of public academic material among government officials. Corruption in education is defined by Hallak and Poisson as:

> The systematic use of public office for private benefit, whose impact is significant on the availability and quality of public goods and services and, as a consequence on access, quality or equity in education. (Hallak and Poisson 2007, p. 29)

Corrupt practices, however, are not limited to public institutions alone. In fact, the growing number of private higher education providers does not reduce corrupt practices but rather increases them due to the less regulated nature of the private sector. Decentralization and privatization increase the incidence of corruption due to the move from 'vertical hierarchies of authority to the horizontal structures of inter- and intra-organisational relations' (Osipian 2007, p. 328).

Studies have also documented the complex relationship between corruption and poverty (World Bank 2000). The Philippines, which ranks 105th out of 174 countries in the corruption index surveyed by Transparency International (2012), has a number of shares in such case. Unfortunately, corruption is likewise prevalent in the poorest region of the country – the Autonomous Region of Muslim Mindanao (ARMM). According to the latest available data on poverty incidence among families (year 2012), ARMM displays the highest poverty rate, at 46.7 per cent (compared to the country's 22.3 per cent). The 2006 Human Development Index (HDI) shows that five of the poorest seven provinces in the country are located in ARMM. Some of the component indices in the HDI consist of secondary school graduation ratio, basic education enrolment rates and life expectancy. The Net Enrolment Ratio (NER) for ARMM is also the lowest in the country, at 71.9 per cent, compared to the country's 88.9 per cent. The same holds true for secondary education, which estimates ARMM at 33.7 per cent compared to the country's 61.2 per cent

(NSCB 2012a; NEDA 2010). The said region consists of five provinces (Basilan, Lanao del Sur, Maguindanao, Sulu and Tawi-Tawi), all of which have a predominantly Muslim population. The region has also experienced years of long-standing struggle and conflict between the government and the MNLF and MILF factions,[2] and it remains as one of the main determinants of poverty in the region. The already limited resources of the government meant to address basic services such as education and health have over the years been hollowed by the response to the conflict (NEDA 2010).

Corruption is also established in ARMM, as witnessed through existing political power relations. The fact of political families governing and controlling the provinces from one generation to the next (and not just limited to ARMM) is well known in the Philippines. Political patronage and wealth accumulation through the political system are but some of the causes for such degeneracy. In 2009, the Maguindanao carnage, which resulted in 58 deaths, was blamed primarily on political power struggles between two opposing families. ARMM is also notorious for corruption in the education sector, with its 'ghost' schools, teachers and students. For instance, in Lanao del Sur, 144 schools were registered with the ARMM Department of Education (DepEd) office, which conflicts with the 130 figure from the main DepEd office in Manila. Schools abandoned due to conflict were also listed as 'active' in Basilan and a total of 22,000 registered teachers were documented in the region as opposed to the 20,000 officially hired figures. These traces of corruption have inevitably defrauded the government of billions of pesos (Laude 2012). Across the country, school feeding programmes were also not spared from corruption practices; the government lost about 170 million Php from an overpriced noodle package awarded to a contractor by the Department of Education (Legaspi 2009).

Relevant to the case mentioned above, Heyneman (2004) further notes that corrupt supplies also occur with respect to the failure to raise bids for the design, printing and distribution of education materials, among others. It is well known that the level of sales of such educational materials and supplies requires high yield especially in countries that are mainly dominated by public educational institutions. The failure to control educational procurement often increases the risk of corruption. Singling out educational providers and failed bidding procedures result in an uncompetitive market. As with other industrial products and materials, a single player in a market can raise prices, which, in turn, affects the product's quality and efficiency; the same goes for educational materials.

Corruption particularly in education also affects the social cohesion of the country through the 'tainted' view of a system that is meant to serve the nation. Some of the educational corruption practices mentioned by Heyneman (2004) include corruption in: (a) selection; (b) systems of accreditation; and (c) supplies. For example, showing partiality towards unqualified applicants in turn hinders access by the greater population who may be better qualified. In effect, this also results in inequity among ethnic or poorer members of societies with regard to fair admission procedures. Furthermore, 'it [corruption] undermines the sources from which countries select future leaders (…), it diminishes the effectiveness … and inhibits access for the poor" (Rumyantseva 2005, p. 84). Since education is seen as a vehicle for human capital development, corruption in such institutions undermines the trust of the general public in educational institutions.

In relation to the Philippines, Azfar and Gurgur (n.d.) reported that corruption in the country weakens health and education services delivery. And in a country challenged by corruption, the prevalence of underweight children under five years of age in 2011 was 20.2 per cent, still missing the Philippines Development Plan (PDP) target of 12.7 per cent for 2016. Similarly for the proportion (66.9 per cent) of households with per capita intake below 100 per cent, dietary energy requirement falls short of the expected PDP target of 32.8 per cent (NSCB 2012b). Corruption is also said to affect all educational outcomes, from test scores, school rankings to satisfaction ratings. Kang (2002) further suggested that corruption and bandwagoning in the Philippines have resulted in missing overall domestic stability and that 'Philippine politics has been dominated by a pendulum of corruption that swung to and fro, but never reached an equilibrium where corruption was constrained … [t]ransaction costs were higher in the Philippines, stability lower, and the economy less efficient' (p. 26).

Policies set for improving educational outcomes

Aware of the inextricable link between education and poverty (Sen 1999), the Philippine government has set up a number of initiatives in line with poverty alleviation through educational development. Particularly for the ARMM area, advancing basic service provision such as access to education, promoting technical vocational education and providing stronger local government unit support for community health and nutrition are being pushed (NEDA 2010). The government has also recognized the need to preserve culture and faith in the region, with the emphasis on support for the local *Madaris* (Islamic schools) and introducing indigenous learning systems that are culturally sensitive. More investments in the secondary level are also envisioned especially in rural areas (NEDA 2010, p. 22). Nutrition services for all are prioritized at the same time, for both the mainstream and internally displaced people. The government has maintained that education campaigns at the local level 'shall focus on reducing malnutrition while limiting the usual strategy of constant government dole-outs through its feeding programme' (ibid., p. 23). Most importantly, there is promotion of 'inclusive peace' through the inclusion of the least developed communities and the marginalized (e.g. disabled, children) to access basic services such as education and health. Social protection programmes for indigents, such as ex-combatants, through the government-sponsored health insurance and coverage are also being pursued (NEDA 2010). The *Bangsamoro*[3] political entity is also envisioned by the government to replace the current ARMM by 2016. This stems part of the Framework Agreement on the Bangsamoro signed by the Philippines government and the Moro Islamic Liberation Front (MILF) in 2012.

On the national scale, the government started the Conditional Cash Transfer (CCT) programme in 2008 with the aim of reaching the poorest of the poor by providing a cash allowance to families 'on condition' that they will participate in programmes that will empower them, such as sending their children to school and having regular health centre visits. This programme is aimed at promoting inclusive growth by supporting human development through improved access to basic services (i.e. health and education). The CCT serves as an alternative to less than effective programmes in poverty alleviation through its supposed long-term human capital investment and immediate shorter-spanned social assistance through its policy emphasis on the use of market-oriented demand-side interventions to directly support the poor (Rawlings and Rubio 2005, p. 29). The CCT programme is well documented in literature, with evidenced success in other countries, and with this logic the Philippine government has re-orientated its poverty alleviation agenda through the implementation of the CCT. Rawlings and Rubio (2005) have documented evidenced success in CCT relating to education and health programmes across Colombia, Nicaragua, Mexico, Honduras, Jamaica and Turkey. They further attributed such success to the advancement of programmes from traditional plans such as CCTs through (a) providing grants directly to poor households, thereby changing accountability relationships among the national government, service providers and the poor (thus strengthening the relationship between the service provider and the poor); (b) seeking to develop complementarities between elements of human capital through their inclusion of health, nutrition and education components and; (c) incorporating strong technical design features that include robust monitoring and evaluation measures (p. 33).

The Conditional Cash Transfer Programme of the government (also known as the *Pantawid Pamiliang Pilipino* Programme or 4Ps) runs with the dual objective of promoting social assistance and development by reaching the poorest communities and breaking the intergenerational cycle of poverty in the country. The plan also aims to help achieve the Philippines' commitment to the Millennium Development Goals through (a) eradicating extreme poverty and hunger; (b) achieving universal primary education; (c) promoting gender equality; (d) reducing child mortality and; (e) improving maternal health (DSWD 2013). Households that are classified as poor by the National Households Targeting System and which have children aged 0–14 and/or a pregnant woman at the time of assessment are eligible to enrol under the programme. The programme has close to 4 million registered households as of 2013 and a proposed 62.6 billion Php for 2014 (Esguerra and Cabacungan 2013). Under the CCT, some of the 'conditionals' that are set to have a direct effect on education access are (DSWD, 2013):

a. 0–5–year-old children must receive regular preventive health check-ups and vaccines;
b. 3–5-year-old children must attend day care or pre-school classes at least 85 per cent of the time.
c. 6–14-year-old children must enrol in elementary or high school and must attend at least 85 per cent of the time.

Additionally, in 2013, the Department of Education has teamed up with the Department of Social Welfare and Development to initiate the mobile 'carton classrooms' as part of the 'revised 4Ps', which aims at reaching the poor communities through mobile makeshift classrooms containing educational resources. Ironically, government offices exert time and effort on projects that can competently be run by apposite non-governmental organizations (NGOs), which the country has aplenty, instead of focusing on actual investments in classrooms and other shortages of the sector. Nevertheless, the CCT programme is said to meet most of its primary objectives. School enrolment for young children has improved and the drop-out rates have diminished. The programme has also achieved its purpose of having poor mothers acquire basic health services and poor pregnant women attending to ante- and post-natal care. Child health has also improved by reducing severe stunting of children aged 6–36 months. However, there are still some areas that need improvement, such as advancing appropriate-age school enrolment among the poor and improving school enrolment for older children (12–17 years), among others (World Bank 2013).

A number of programmes launched by the Department of Education cater to ensuring that malnutrition, one of the major effects of poverty, is addressed in schools. The Breakfast Feeding Programme (BFP) was initially launched in 1997 to address issues of short-term hunger experienced by public school children as a result of skipping breakfast and walking long distances to reach schools (Meniano 2012). Today, it is not uncommon to observe feeding programmes in schools that aim to provide additional sustenance for students, especially those who come from poor communities. Schools usually have their own gardens where vegetables and other plants are grown to add to such feeding programmes. It is estimated that more than half million children suffer from malnutrition (Delfin 2013) and that children ranked third in terms of poverty incidence (in 2009), just falling behind fishermen and farmers, who top the list (NSCB 2013). Recently, the Department of Education targeted more than 40,000 severely wasted school children with their feeding programme with the aim of improving their health and school performance, assuming the link between academic under-performance and hunger (PIA 2013). Also, given the varied topography of the country, it is not unusual to hear of students having to travel long distances to reach schools (Symaco 2013), which also explains hunger and lack of attention during school hours. These feeding programmes, however, do not guarantee a comprehensive alternative, given the lack of resources also faced by schools in the country.

Poverty in practice: Grassroots realities

Do stakeholders' perceptions matter anyway? When we identify 'stakeholders' as the actual poor, this links to the set of actions displayed by such individuals as it relates to their initiatives and life decisions in determining their own realities. Jervis (1976) distinguishes between the 'psychological milieu' and the 'operational milieu', respectively corresponding to how people perceive the world and the world in which policies of institutions are carried out. He further underlines how 'stakeholders' influence realities according to their goals, calculations and perceptions. It is often futile to analyse a stakeholder's decision without referring to and studying his beliefs, opinions and perceptions (Yee 1996).

> When I came to Manila, I barely had anything and life in the province was better but I was willing to gamble with the idea of possibly having a better future with the chances of finding work [in Manila]. My life in the province would still be better as compared to what I have now in the city but I still prefer to stay in the city with the opportunities that it has to offer which is lacking in my province. For me, poverty is the lack of opportunities and not just a lack of having a place to live.[4]

Two subsidiary issues concerning perception emerge here: one is whether important decisions are derived from different perceptions of 'stakeholders' and the other is whether there are significant differences between common and shared perceptions and reality. This translates and relates to perception, for instance, as viewed by individuals resolving to move from rural areas, as exemplified above, to urban areas with the desire to obtain work. When people from such areas choose to leave their comfort zones in search of better living, does their definition of a 'better life' or 'out of poverty' actually translate to what one would normally expect?

> My children were not able to finish school because of poverty. We do not have enough money to pay for school expenses. It would've been ideal to finish schooling and to find a proper paying job but given our limitation, the only option is to ask my children to stop going to school and help the family earn a living. For others, going to school means having a better life. We believe this too, but with our own realities, a 'better life' simply means earning just enough to survive the day.[5]

Blumer (1969) recounts that the interpretation by individuals of others has considerable significance in studying social actions and interactions:

> It is important to see how this process of designation and interpretation is sustaining, undercutting, redirecting, and transforming the ways in which participants are fitting together their lines of action. (Blumer 1969, p. 53)

The behaviour, therefore, of individuals is seen in terms of the 'lines of actions' of others with whom they are interacting. The fact that people in the same situation often react to and perceive things differently is a paradigm that shows the importance of considering how the poor actually perceive 'poverty' – specifically as to how deeply they are convinced that it is vital in their life choices (to go to school or to quit school?). It is also important to know how education plays a part (otherwise) in their 'desire to move out of poverty'.

Wasserman and Faust (1994) and Rowley (1997) make use of social systems theory and relations to 'understand social actions and phenomena' because 'relationships do not exist in a dyadic vacuum but through a network of influences' (as cited in Symaco 2013b, p. 137). It is, therefore, important to understand the multifaceted and interdependent relationships subsisting between and among stakeholders themselves. In this way, it provides a 'mechanism for conceptualising the simultaneous influence of multiple stakeholders [as opposed to individual stakeholders] and predicting organisational response to these forces' (Symaco, 2013b, 888). In relation to education and poverty alleviation, taking note of grassroots perspectives will also prevent the introduction of policies that are detached from actual reality. With local definitions and realities in mind, solutions proposed are authenticated as relevant across the social unit. Given the excerpts above, it is evident that 'poverty' is defined beyond merely the ability to have basic shelter, and that education, though considered as a solution to poverty, may not be accessed when the priority, ironically, is to avoid an empty stomach.

Closing remarks

This chapter discussed the issues of poverty and malnutrition in the Philippines, and the significant role of education as perceived by the Philippine government in resolving such challenges. As mentioned earlier, it is important to take into consideration the interrelated functions of the different sectors of society when addressing issues relating to poverty. The dynamic and interconnected role, for instance, of education and health is exemplified through the ability of individuals to optimize educational outcomes as they suit their health condition. Students who attend school with empty stomachs fail to be attentive to their lessons in class, while students who often come from poor large families tend to drop out due to the responsibility to help their families earn a living (Symaco 2011; Symaco 2013a). Proper governance is also important to address as corruption leads to unequal opportunities. As mentioned by Hallak and Poisson (2007) in relation to education, the use of

UNIVERSITY OF WINCHESTER LIBRARY

private 'benefit' of individuals over a public system can undermine the quality, access and equity of the education sector.

The importance of considering the grassroots approach in terms of implementing education and poverty alleviation programmes is also addressed. Education, when used properly, can be an effective factor in improving human capacities. As Sen (1999) observes, its relevance in directly influencing the well-being of people and indirectly through its role in effecting social change, education is a powerful tool in enhancing the conditions of people, particularly the poor. It is vital though to be aware of the actual situations of the poor, as perceived through the grassroots approach, as new opportunities and policies should operate in line with the local context so that we build on the realities of the community. As Carr (2008, p. 733) notes, it is then that 'we develop critical understandings of what works … develop and augment responses that build resilience for all, and not just a few'.

Questions for reflection

a. How are education and poverty linked? How can education help in the formation or alleviation of poverty and how can poverty affect educational outcomes?

b. When we say that sectors (e.g. education and health) are interdependent and that compartmentalizing them runs the risk of failing to address poverty alleviation, what do we mean by this?

c. How can a government in general, and the Philippine government in particular, improve its sectors to ensure the optimal use of education for development?

Notes

1   1 US dollars = approximately 43 Philippine pesos.

2   MNLF and MILF stands for Moro National Liberation Front and the Moro Islamic Liberation Front, respectively. A long-standing warfare has been waged against the Philippine government due to conflicting ancestral domain claims. Refer to Symaco and Baunto (2010) for more details.

3   *Bangsamoro* refers to (Muslim) people who are known natives of parts of Sabah (now Malaysia), Mindanao, Palawan and the Sulu archipelago in the Philippines. The term is used to coin the Filipino Muslim (*Moro*) and national identity (*Bangsa*) (Milligan 2006).

4   Interviews translated from Filipino to English.

5   Interviews translated from Filipino to English.

Further reading

1. Bourdieu, P and Passeron, J (1977) *Reproduction in Education, Society and Culture*. London: Sage Publications.

    This book gives a critical theory of social reproduction and investigates the dynamic relationship between education (not merely confined to the formal setting) and class groups.

2. Symaco, L.P. (2013). Geographies of social exclusion: education access in the Philippines. *Comparative Education, 49*(3), 361–373.

    This article examines education access in the Philippines and focuses on some of the most remote and conflict-ridden areas in the country. It discusses the role of poverty and non-access to mainstream services, such as education, as experienced by the communities in question.

3. Symaco, L.P. and Baunto, A. (2010). Islamic education in the Philippines with reference to issues of access and mobility. *The International Journal of Educational and Psychological Assessment, 5*(2), 223–236.

    This article gives a good overview of Islamic education in the Philippines. Factors contributing to the failure to enhance human potential among the Filipino Muslims, such as poverty and the effects of conflict in Southern Philippines, are also discussed.

References

ADB (2009). *Poverty in the Philippines: Causes, Constraints and Opportunities*. Pasig: ADB.

Ahrens, L. and McNamara, V. (2013). Cambodia: evolving quality issues in higher education. In L. P. Symaco (Ed.) *Education in South East*. London/New York Bloomsbury Publishing, 47–69.

Azfar, O. and Gurgur, T. (n.d.). Does Corruption Affect Health and Education Outcomes in the Philippines? Available at: http://unpan1.un.org/intradoc/groups/public/documents/APCITY/UNPAN024529.pdf [accessed 6 July 2013].

Bardhan, P. (1996). Equity and poverty alleviation: policy issues in less developed countries. *The Economic Journal, 106*(438), 1344–1356.

Blumer, H. (1969). *Symbolic Interactionism: Perspectives from Government, Education and Business*. Las Vegas: University of Nevada.

Boughton, B. (2013). Timor-Leste education, decolonisation and development. In L. P. Symaco (Ed.). *Education in South East Asia*. London/ New York: Bloomsbury Publishing, 299–321.

Brock, C. and Symaco, L. P. (2011). *Education in South East Asia*. Oxford: Symposium Books.

Carr, E. (2008). Rethinking poverty alleviation: a 'poverties' approach. *Development in Practice, 18*(6), 726–734.

CIA (2013). *The World Factbook*. Available at: https://www.cia.gov/library/publications/the-world-factbook//fields/2177.html [accessed 28 June 2013].

Delfin, C. (2013). *More than Half Million Pinoy Kids Suffer from Severe Malnutrition*. Available at: http://www.gmanetwork.com/news/story/296884/news/specialreports/more-than-half-million-pinoy-kids-suffer-from-severe-malnutrition [accessed 26 July 2013].

DSWD (2013). *The Pantawid Pamilyang Pilipino Program.* Available at: http://pantawid.dswd.gov.ph/index.php/about-us [accessed 15 July 2013].

Esguerra, C. and Cabacungan, G. (2013). *2014 National Budget.* Available at: http://newsinfo.inquirer.net/452247/p27b-pork-in-2014-national-budget [accessed 10 August 2013].

Executive Order 69 (2012). *Strengthening the Presidential Commission for the Urban Poor.* Manila: Office of the President.

Hallak, J. and Poisson, M. (2002). *Ethics and Corruption in Education.* Paris: IIEP.

—— (2007). *Corrupt Schools, Corrupt Universities: What Can Be Done?* Paris: IIEP.

Harbison, F. and Myers, C. (1964). Education and employment in the newly developing economies. *Comparative Education Review, 8*(1), 5–10.

Hayden, M. and Le, N. L. (2013). Vietnam: the education system – a need to improve quality. In L. P. Symaco (Ed.). *Education in South East Asia.* London/New York: Bloomsbury Publishing, 323–344.

Heyneman, S. (2004). Education and corruption. *International Journal of Educational Development, 24*(6), 637–648.

Iredale, R. (2001). The migration of professionals: theories and typologies. *International Migration, 39*(5), 7–26.

Jervis, R. (1976). *Perception and Misperception in International Politics.* New Jersey: Princeton University Press.

Kang, D. (2002). *Transaction Costs and Crony Capitalism in East Asia.* Available at: http://papers.ssrn.com/sol3/papers.cfm?abstract_id=310592 [accessed 6 July 2013].

Laude, J. (2012). *Ghost students, Ghost Teachers, Ghost schools Haunt ARMM.* Available at: http://www.philstar.com/breaking-news/802552/ghost-students-ghost-teachers-ghost-schools-haunt-armm [accessed 6 July 2013].

Legaspi, A. (2009). *DepEd Suspends Contract of Supplier of 'overpriced' Noodles.* Available at: http://www.gmanetwork.com/news/story/160881/news/nation/deped-suspends-contract-of-supplier-of-overpriced-noodles [accessed 6 July 2013].

Melin, M. (2001). *Education- A Way Out of Poverty?* Stockholm: SIDA.

Meniano, S. (2012). *DepEd to Pursue Breakfast Feeding Programme.* Available at: http://leytesamardaily.net/2012/06/deped-to-pursue-breakfast-feeding-program/ [accessed 26 July 2013].

Milligan, J. (2006). Reclaiming an ideal: The Islamization of education in the Southern Philippines. *Comparative Education Review, 50*(3), 410–430.

Mohd Asri, MN (2012). Advancing the orang asli through Malaysia's clusters of excellence policy. *Journal of International and Comparative Education, 1*(2), 90–103.

NEDA (2010). *Mindanao Strategic Development Framework 2010–2020.* Pasig: NEDA.

Noonan, R. (2011). Education in the Lao People's Democratic Republic: confluence of history and vision. In C. Brock and L. P. Symaco (Eds). *Education in South East Asia.* Oxford: Symposium Books, 69–94.

NSCB (2012a). *Low School Enrolment Ratios: Will K-12 Help or Will it Push the Ratios Even Lower?* Available at: http://www.nscb.gov.ph/sexystats/2012/SS20120620_enrolment.asp#tab2 [accessed 15 July 2013].

———— (2012b). *Statistical Indicators on Philippine Development*. Available at: http://www.nscb.gov.ph/stats/statdev/2012/ch7_social.asp [accessed 15 July 2013].

———— (2013). *Poverty Incidence Unchanged*. Available at: http://www.nscb.gov.ph/poverty/defaultnew.asp [accessed 6 July 2013].

Osipian, A. (2007). Corruption in higher education: conceptual approaches and measurement technique. *Research in Comparative and International Education*, 2(4), 313–332.

Pham, LH and Fry, G. (2011). Vietnam as an outlier: traditions and change in education. In C. Brock and L. P. Symaco (Eds). *Education in South East Asia*. Oxford: Symposium Books, 221–243.

PIA (2013). *Feeding Programme*. Available at: http://www.pia.gov.ph/news/index.php?article=1781358387651 [accessed 26 July 2013].

Raffo, C., Dyson, A., Gunter, H., Hall, D., Jones, L. and Kalambouka, A. (2009). Education and poverty: mapping the terrain and making the links to educational policy. *International Journal of Inclusive Education*, 13(4), 341–358.

Rawlngs, L. and Rubio, G. (2005). Evaluating the impact of conditional cash transfer programs. *The World Bank Observer*, 20(1), 29–55.

Rowley, T. (1997). Moving beyond dyadic ties: a network theory of stakeholder influences. *Academy of Management Review*, 14(7), 325–333.

Rumyantseva, N. (2005). Taxonomy of corruption in higher education. *Peabody Journal of Education*, 80(1), 81–92.

Sen, A. (1999). *Development as Freedom*. Oxford: Oxford University Press.

Symaco, L. P. (2010). Higher education and equity in Malaysia. *International Journal of Educational and Psychological Assessment*, 5(2), 265–272.

———— (2011). Philippines: Education for development? In C. Brock and L. P. Symaco (Eds) *Education in South East Asia*. Oxford: Symposium Books, 139–155.

———— (2012). Higher education in the Philippines and Malaysia: the learning region in the age of knowledge-based societies. *Journal of International and Comparative Education*, 1(1). Available at: http://crice.um.edu.my/downloads/symaco.pdf [accessed 4 July 2013].

———— (2013). Geographies of social exclusion: education access in the Philippines, *Comparative Education*, 49(3), 361–373.

———— (2013a). *Education in South East Asia*. London/New York: Bloomsbury Publishing.

———— (2013b). Education in the knowledge-based society: the case of the Philippines. *Asia Pacific Journal of Education*, 33(2), 183–196.

Thurow, L. (1967). The causes of poverty. *The Quarterly Journal of Economics*, 81(1), 39–57.

Transparency International (2012). *Corruption Perceptions Index 2012*. Available at: http://www.transparency.org/cpi2012/results [accessed 15 July 2013].

UNDP (1997). *Human Development Report*. New York: UNDP.

UNFP (2012). *The State of World Population 2012*. New York: UNFP.

UNICEF (2007). *Child Poverty in Perspective: An Overview of Child Well-being in Rich Countries*. Florence: UNICEF.

Van der Berg, S. (2008). *Poverty and Education*. Available at: http://www.iiep.unesco.org/fileadmin/user_upload/Info_Services_Publications/pdf/2009/EdPol10.pdf [accessed 28 June 2013].

Wasserman, S. and Faust, K. (1994). *Structural Analysis in the Social Sciences*. Cambridge: Cambridge University Press.

Welch, A. (2013). Different paths, one goad: Southeast Asia as a knowledge society. *Asia Pacific Journal of Education*, *33*(2), 212–221.

Wikeley, F., K. Bullock, Y. Muschamp, and Ridge, T. (2008). Educational relationships and their impact on poverty. *International Journal of Inclusive Education*, *13*(4), 377–393.

World Bank (2000). *Combating Corruption in the Philippines*, Washington D.C.: World Bank.

——(2013). *Cash Conditional Transfers Pay Off in the Philippines*. Available at: http://www.worldbank.org/en/news/feature/2013/06/10/conditional-cash-transfers-pay-off-in-the-philippines [accessed 26 July 2013].

Yee, A. (1996). The causal effects of idea on policies. *International Organization*, *50*(1), 69–108.

School, Poverty and Hunger in the UK

Rys Farthing

7

Introduction

The UK has enjoyed 'free at the point of delivery' school education since 1944 (*Education Act 1944*), and by and large, all British children enjoy access to this. According to the latest data, 100 per cent of children in the UK are enrolled in primary school (World Bank 2010) and on top of this, by 2015 participation in education or training will be compulsory for all young people up to the age of 18 (*Education and Skills Act 2008*). This means that the vast majority of British young people will complete both primary and secondary education. Yet despite this education for all, a number of disadvantaged children across Britain remain marginalized within the school system.

So while very few young people are actively 'excluded' from formal education, many young people from marginalized social groups do not enjoy the same outcomes from, nor the same experience of, school education as their peers. As the UN Committee on the Rights of the Child noted when it last explored the UK's implementation of children's rights

> significant inequalities persist with regard to school achievement of children living with their parents in economic hardship. Several groups of children ... cannot fully

> enjoy their right to education, notably children with disabilities, children of
> Travellers, Roma children, asylum-seeking children, dropouts and non-attendees
> for different reasons (sickness, family obligations etc.), and teenage mothers.
> (Committee on the Rights of the Child 2008, para. 66 and 67)

These young people often have worse outcomes and experiences of education across the UK. If education as a humanitarian response entails delivering an appropriate education for all young people (Brock and McCorriston 2008), then clearly the experiences of these marginalized groups of young people point towards scope for improvement within the UK's seemingly universal formal provision.

While each of these groups will have their own unique experience of what educational marginalization means for them, this chapter aims to unpack and explore the complexity of the relationship between poverty and education within the UK. This is for both the sake of brevity and because, as outlined below, poverty appears to be a common experience shared by many marginalized groups of young people across the UK. While the relationship between poverty and education is complex and often not clear, this chapter aims to provide both a broad overview and to specifically use the example of hunger as a case study of an intermediary factor between low incomes and educational outcomes. Hunger has been selected as a case study to both tie this chapter together with the theme of the book and because it is an especially illustrative case study. Both hunger and poor attainment appear to be features of the experience of growing up poor in the UK, while at the same time, the education system has a central role to play in mitigating both of these consequences of poverty.

Wherever possible, this chapter aims to also present the view from the ground, and offers the thoughts and words of some children and young people themselves. This is in part to highlight the extra complexity of the issue which emerges from moving beyond descriptive survey data to real-world narratives, and in part to realize children and young people's right to be heard in discussions that affect them. These voices and experiences were gathered through both an online survey of young British people and a series of focus groups engaging disadvantaged or marginalized young people living in financially deprived areas across England.

The survey data referred come from a British Youth Council survey of 377 young people from around the UK, conducted in February 2013. Eighty of the young people who participated identified themselves as coming from low income families. The focus group data come from two sources: first, from a series of focus groups conducted by the author in low-income neighbourhoods across England; second, the visual images emerge from a series of focus groups conducted with young people using Kids Company 'drop in' and free dinner services across London (CPAG et al. 2013).

To begin, it is necessary to describe the phenomenon of poverty in the UK, and outline its consequences for young people who live in it.

Education and poverty in the UK

Some 2.3 million children in the UK currently live below the official British poverty line (DWP 2012). While this claim does not reflect the levels of absolute poverty seen in many other parts of the world addressed within this book, it reflects a notion of relative deprivation. As sociologist Peter Townsend described this relative notion of poverty:

> Individuals, families and groups in the population can be said to be in poverty when they lack the resources to obtain the type of diet, participate in the activities and have the living conditions and the amenities which are customary, or at least widely encouraged or approved in the societies to which they belong. Their resources are so seriously below those commanded by the average family that they are in effect excluded from the ordinary living patterns, customs, and activities. (Townsend 1979, p. 31)

Across the UK, as enshrined in the *Child Poverty Act 2010*, this relative deprivation is operationalized as being 60 per cent of median household incomes, equivalized to reflect household size. This is the threshold below which 2.3 million children, or roughly 18 per cent of all British children, live (DWP 2012).

These low incomes produce the type of exclusions that Townsend talks about. For example, 14 per cent of children living in household with the lowest 20 per cent of incomes cannot afford a bicycle or other common children's leisure equipment, while no child in the highest income quintile misses out on daily fruit or veg for want of money (DWP 2012). Likewise, 5 per cent of children in the lowest income quintile cannot afford a warm winter coat, while no child in the highest income quintile misses it out (DWP 2012).

Many marginalized groups of young people also suffer a disproportionately high risk of poverty. As Table 7.1 highlights, the risk of poverty, or the percentage of each group that lives in poverty, is higher for families affected by disability, families from ethnic minorities and single-parent families.

Table 7.1 The risk of poverty for various groups of children, 2010/11 (DWP 2012)

'At risk' group	Risk of poverty, %		Reference group
Families affected by disability			
Those living in families with disabled adults (but no disabled children)	26		
Those living in families with disabled children (but no disabled adults)	18	16	Children living in families where no one is disabled
Those living in families with a disabled adult and a disabled child	20		
Ethnic minorities			
Mixed-race children	26		
Asian or Asian British children	37		
Black or Black British children	30	17	White children
Chinese children or other ethnic group	32		
Family type			
Children living in single-parent families	22	16	Children living in two-parent families

However, Table 7.1 only presents official statistics, and many other marginalized groups are also at higher risk of experiencing poverty despite their absences from official datasets. For example, much anecdotal evidence suggests that a disproportionate number of Gypsy, Roma and Traveller young people live in low income households, an experience which may be institutionally reinforced through restrictions to the benefits system and work permits (Foster and Norton 2012). Second, young people living in care do not necessarily figure in national datasets about child poverty, as official measures collect only information about household income and many of these youngsters live outside of what is statistically defined as a household. Regardless, many of these young people are keen to point out that poverty affects their lives too. As one group of children in care I spoke to described it,

> Poverty is a main driver of why children come in to care. While to an extent, all children in [their area] are vulnerable to poverty…children and young people in care are especially vulnerable to its effects, because they lack the protection of a stable family. (in Farthing 2012a)

Third, the experience of asylum-seeking and refugee young people is also likely to be defined by severe financial hardship. Limited permission to work and extremely low levels of benefits leave many refugee families with far less than enough to meet their basic needs (Williams and Kaye 2010, p. 31). While the lived experience of growing up on a low income will differ between all of these groups of young people, poverty appears to be a central feature to the lives of many marginalized and vulnerable young people around the UK.

Growing up in poverty in the UK has profound impacts on a child's educational attainment. For example, children who are entitled to free school meals in England – a rough, proxy measure for poverty, as discussed below – are 17 per cent less likely to achieve good grades by age 11 (DfE 2013a). This gap continues into secondary school, where children receiving free school meals are 26 per cent less likely to receive good grades at age 16, and 25 per cent less likely to have obtained the expected level of school-leavers qualifications by their 19th birthday (DfE 2013b). This attainment gap has knock-on consequences for young people's participation in higher education. In 2010 for example, only 18 per cent of children on free school meals went on higher or further education, half as many when compared to the 36 per cent of young people not in receipt of free school meals who entered higher education (Department for Business Innovation and Skill 2012).

When compared to other 'developed' (OECD – Organisation for Economic Cooperation and Development) nations, this link between students' socio-economic background and educational attainment is greater than expected in the UK. Data from the latest PISA survey showed that the UK had the 27th highest level of inequality of outcome for students from socio-economically disadvantaged backgrounds for reading, out of 34 OECD nations (OECD 2010). That is, in the UK, an individual student's socio-economic background has a greater impact on their performance than in most other OECD nations. It is worth noting, however, that the same survey shows that mainly because of the low levels of socio-economic disadvantage in the UK, the amount of variance across student performance that can be explained by disadvantage in the UK is, overall, on par with the OECD norm (OECD 2010).

This mixed picture tells its own story; from a national perspective the UK's education system appears to be doing well, but from the perspective of a low income student, however, the education system presents a number of unique challenges. But from this view from the ground, from a young person's perspective, the picture becomes clouded. As the British children from low income households I have spoken to are keen to remind us, the statistical landscape described above does not necessarily mean that every young person growing up in a low income household is doomed to educational underperformance. Poverty is not necessarily deterministic, and many young people thrive in school despite their poverty; otherwise, no student on free school meals would achieve good grades. Figure 7.1 suggests this is not the case; it is less likely, but not impossible, for a student from a low income family to do well in school. As Tamara and Keila put it when I spoke to them:

> Tamara: 'It says like, I saved in on my phone, the [newspaper article]. It says like how poor we are and like how we grow up like ... '
> Keila: 'Like little feral kids.'
> Tamara: 'Like we've got nothing, like, lost in our own. But like every kid [around here] makes their own decisions'. (Farthing, forthcoming)

Both Tamara and Keila have since enrolled in university.

The links between poverty and attainment described above are only one, albeit consequential, aspect of the relationship between poverty and education for young people in Britain. Growing up in poverty in the UK also impacts on young people's ability to participate in, and enjoy their time at, school.

Participating in a formal education in the UK, despite the school's being free at the point of delivery, still costs. For many young people, the cost of

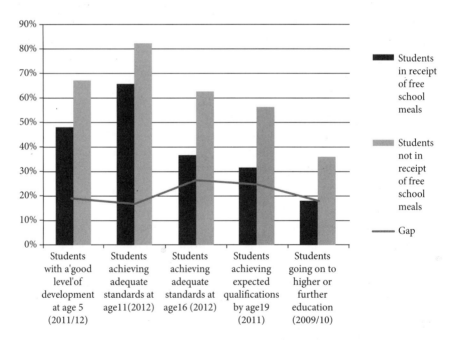

Figure 7.1 Educational attainment in England by free school meal status and age (DfE 2013ab, BIS 2012)

purchasing uniforms, books, materials and school trips proves difficult. The average spends on these items tallied £1,195 (approx. USD $1800) per student in secondary school, and £684 (USD $1000) per primary school student in 2007 (Peters et al. 2009). Tellingly, low income families still made sure these costs were met. Families living on incomes below £15,000 per annum (USD $23,000) still spent on average £647 ($978, or 95 per cent of the average spend) per primary school student and £1117 ($1690 or 95 per cent of the average spend) per secondary school student (Peters et al. 2009, p. 35). This represents a Herculean effort by these families to put aside at least 4 per cent of their annual income per primary school student and 7 per cent per secondary school student to cover these costs.

However, despite the effort not all of the costs of a school education can be met for low income young people in the UK. Nine per cent of children from households with the lowest 20 per cent of incomes cannot afford to go on a school trip once a term, for example, while no young person from the top 20 per cent misses out due to cost (DWP 2012). Many young people living in low income families exclude themselves from these educational activities and opportunities because of the costs; some 7 per cent of children living in families with annual incomes below £15,000 per year do not take notes home to their parents about trips because they know they cannot afford them (Peters et al. 2009, p. 157).

Missing out on school trips made available to other students has a huge impact on poorer students' education, as well as on their ability to make friends at school. As two young people from low income families surveyed suggested:

> It was unfair … I missed out on valuable experience and Italian speaking skills and also I missed out on a chance to go on holiday with my class mates. I felt separated when they got back because they all had stories to tell
>
> It made making new friends difficult as (I missed) the year 7 residential. (CPAG et al. 2013)

Students from lower income families also talk about not being able to enjoy the full curriculum made available to other students at school. For example, students from low income families surveyed suggested that taking subjects that require additional spends on materials – often creative subjects such as art, photography or cooking – was not a viable option for them.

> Purchasing extra materials has always been an issue. For me I only choose those lessons I didn't had to spend too much money on them. (CPAG et al. 2013)

Where they do take these subjects, they often feel unable to perform well:

> I have regretted [picking photography] since, and wish I had taken a different subject instead. The demand for providing my own materials is high, and there are times I have been penalised for not having photos printed because I don't have the necessary equipment, or not got sketchbooks, etc. (CPAG et al. 2013)

As the young person above suggests, there is an expectation among teachers that the basic costs of schooling can be met, so students who cannot meet them are often regarded as personally deviant. For example, a student who could not afford to replace his worn-out school blazer told me that 'it has a huge effect [on his education] because instead of teachers teaching you'd get told off for your uniform' (CPAG et al. 2013).

Similarly, students without access to a computer within their home are disadvantaged. One student suggested that not having a personal computer had 'a big impact because teachers expected all homework either printed out or on a USB stick, so [she had] to get a train into the next town along just to use their library computers because [the town's local] library got shut down'. Not having enough money to cover the costs of schooling in the UK means that students are missing out on the curriculum opportunities their richer peers can afford (Figure 7.2).

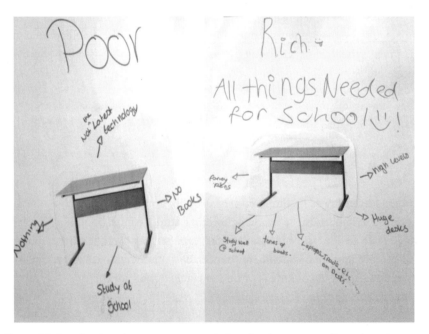

Figure 7.2 Drawing done by some young people from low income areas illustrating what 'poor' and 'rich' children have to help them study at home

Aside from being unable to participate in the curriculum for want of money, poverty also impacts on young people's school attendance. Students who are eligible for Free School Meals (FSM) – a proxy indicator for poverty – miss an average of 7.3 per cent of school half days, compared to 4.5 per cent of half days missed by their richer peers (DfE 2012a). Beyond temporary absences, young people eligible for FSM were almost four times more likely to be permanently excluded (or expelled) from school than their better-off peers, and three times more likely to be temporarily excluded (suspended) (DfE 2012b).

These lower levels of engagement may in part reflect some deeper disenchantment with school. And such disenchantment and dislike of school may begin very early. For example, a study of 10- and 11-year-old boys in Northern Ireland (Horgan 2007) highlighted how students attending schools in areas with high levels of disadvantage complained that they were shouted at by teachers, a complaint not replicated in more advantaged schools. Likewise, a study by Sutton et al. (2007) found that students from financially deprived neighbourhoods felt they were shouted at for not knowing what to do, and generally described school a controlling and coercive environment.

Interviewer: 'Is life more unfair to some children than others?'
Girl 1: 'Yes, it is. It's unfair for us (young people from a deprived neighborhood) because we have to just listen to teachers all the time.'
Interviewer: 'But isn't that the same for all children?'
Girl 2: 'No. It's not, because if you're rich you get to go to a posh school where the teachers probably teach you with respect'. (Sutton et al. 2007, p. 21)

For these young people, perhaps unsurprisingly, skipping lessons and 'wagging' classes were talked about with a sense of pride (Sutton et al. 2007).

Additionally, many young people from low income neighbourhoods attend government-funded schools that are, simply put, not as good as the ones their better-off peers attend. All government-funded schools in the UK are assessed annually, and the assessment body notes a 'marked inequality of access to a good school across the country' (Ofstead 2012, p. 7), which corresponds strongly with regional deprivation. Students living in the most deprived areas have a 20–25 per cent chance of attending a school rated 'outstanding', and a 35–40 per cent chance of attending a 'satisfactory or inadequate' school (the lowest rating) (Clifton and Cook 2012). Contrastingly, students from the least deprived areas have a 35–45 per cent chance of attending an 'outstanding' school and only a 20–25 per cent chance of attending a school assessed to be only 'satisfactory or inadequate' (Clifton and Cook 2012). Put simply, 'pupils from deprived areas are about as likely to attend a school rated "satisfactory" or "inadequate" as wealthier pupils are to attend a school rated as "outstanding"' (Clifton and Cook 2012, p.20).

Young people growing up in low income households in the UK often do not perform as well, nor attend as often, nor attend the same calibre of, nor enjoy school as much as their richer peers. Despite a 'free at the point of delivery' universal school system, young people from low income households still pay to go to school, but often cannot afford to meet these costs fully. They are more likely to be suspended or expelled, and do not enjoy school as much as their richer peers. They are also more likely to attend inadequate schools. In short, Britain's school system has scope to improve in its provision of an appropriate education for all young people, and to ensure all British children enjoy their right to an education equally.

Hunger and poverty in the UK

The experience of growing up poor in the UK is often punctuated by hunger and a poor diet. Individuals in households in the lowest 20 per cent of incomes consume on average only 1900 calories per day – 5 per cent fewer calories than people on average incomes – and less than the daily recommended allowance (Food Statistics Unit 2012). They also purchase few portions of fruit and vegetables per day, consuming around 3 servings per day compared to the 4 per day of people in average households, well below the recommended 5 portions (Food Statistics Unit 2012). Figure 7.3 highlights the strong relationship between income and fruit and vegetable purchases in the UK.

While overall, the total amount of food purchased in low income households may be less than average, food remains a big-ticket spend in these households. Households with the lowest 20 per cent of incomes spent 16.6 per cent of their weekly income on food in 2011, compared to 11.3 per cent in average income household (Food Statistics Unit 2012). In short, a large 'chunk of change' gets spent of food where families are surviving on low income.

This leaves families on low incomes in the UK extremely sensitive to increases in food price. For example, since 2007 when food prices began to increase in the UK above inflation, families on all incomes, but especially those on lower incomes, began to purchase fewer fruits and fewer vegetables as a result (Food Statistics Unit 2012). Figure 7.4 highlights that since the spike in food prices in 2007, households of all incomes have decreased their purchase of vegetables by 4.4 per cent (Food Statistics Unit 2012). However, households in the lowest decile have decreased further, by 12 per cent, and households in

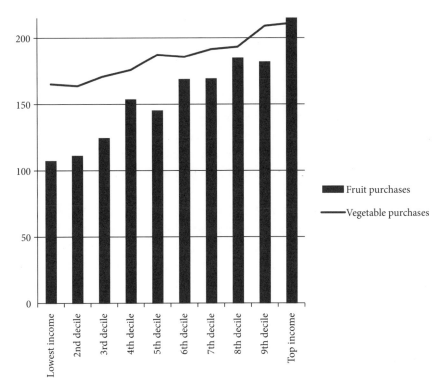

Figure 7.3 The average grams of fruit and vegetables purchased by household income in the UK, 2011 (Food Statistics Unit 2012)

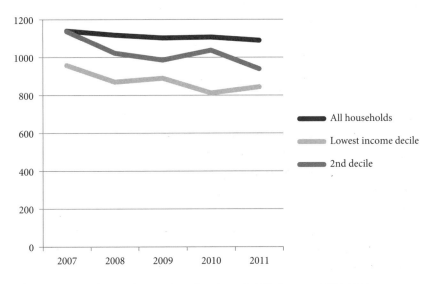

Figure 7.4 Grams of vegetables purchased per household by income, 2007–2011 (Food Statistics Unit 2012)

the second poorest decile have decreased by 17 per cent. For the second income decile, where they were previously consuming almost the same amount of vegetables as average income households, they have since fallen well behind on their vegetable consumption.

While the data above all describe diets for whole low income households, this link between income and healthy diet also plays out for young people. Eight per cent of children living in the lowest income decile and 5 per cent of children living in the second lowest income decile cannot afford fresh fruit or vegetables everyday, while none in the highest income decile misses out for want of money (DWP 2012).

Hunger and a poor diet have an impact on a child's ability to participate in education. Being nutritionally deprived while below school age has the ability to reduce cognitive outcomes when they become school-aged. For example, being B12 deficient in early life reduces cognitive test scores in adolescence (in Sorhaindo and Feinstein 2006, p. 12). Beyond these long-term consequences, nutrition can have more immediate impacts on children's behaviour, such as concentration or the ability to interact with peers. For example, a diet low in vitamin B appears to be related to behavioural problems such aggression in adolescence (Bellisle 2004).

But perhaps the most commonly understood relationship is that between hunger and concentration. As many parents can tell you, children who are hungry struggle to concentrate, and clinical studies show that an adequate supply of glucose to the brain enhances cognitive functioning (Benton 2001). As Sorhaindo and Feinstein (2006, p. i) outlined, 'maintaining adequate levels of glucose throughout the day contributes to optimising cognition'. In short, children need to eat properly to learn well.

This link – between hunger and learning – was recognized by the British government over a century ago. In 1906 they passed the *Education (Provision of Meals) Act*, which gave local education authorities the capacity to provide meals to children who were 'unable by reason of lack of food to take full advantage of the education provided for them'. This led to the creation of a Free School Meal scheme which has continued to the present day. This FSM scheme ensures that free lunches are made available to children living in low income, predominantly workless households, at schools.

FSMs now play an important part in meeting the nutritional needs of 1.2 million young people (DfE 2012c) in the UK. Strict nutritional standards apply to all school meals provided in the UK, so that they are healthy and balanced. Food and nutrition standards for school meals are legislated, and require a combination of healthy food groups to be provided throughout a school week. They limit the amount of fatty and sugary foods and ensure that lunches must provide at least one-third of most daily recommendations for nutrients (The Education (Nutritional Standards and Requirements for School Food) (England) Regulations 2007). In fact, the regulations and requirements are so stringent that in 2009 only 1 per cent of lunches students brought from home met these standards (Schools Food Trust 2012).

However, there are some limitations to the capacity of this scheme to adequately tackle young people's hunger, four of which this chapter will outline: inadequacy of entitlement; stigma; restrictions to the midday meal; and lack of entitlement over holidays.

First, as outlined above, 1.2 million children are entitled to FSM (DfE 2012c), while some 2.3 million children live in poverty (DWP 2012). While not all of these 2.3 million children living in poverty will be of school age, there is still a clear and present discrepancy between these two figures. In short, not every child living in poverty is entitled to FSM, and research suggests that around 20 per cent of children living below the poverty line are not entitled (London Economics 2008). This is because, generally, entitlement to FSM is linked to parental work status (CPAG 2012). Children of unemployed parents are entitled to FSM, but not those whose parents are in low paid or part time work, who still live below the poverty line. Some 60 per cent of children living below the poverty line have at least one parent in work (DWP 2012), so would probably not be entitled to FSM. Many young people perceive this inadequacy as unfair;

> I think … families that are on low income [should also be entitled to FSM] because my friend has two other sisters in a single parent family and has very low income and really struggles to have anything for lunch but doesn't get free school meals. I personally think that this is really unfair. (Young person in Farthing 2012b, p. 12)

But the inadequacy does not stop at entitlement alone. FSMs are often delivered at school in the form of credit or vouchers to spend at the school canteen. Many young people who are on FSM report that they do not get enough credit to actually purchase a full meal, and as a result go hungry:

> There's not enough money allocated to us and I go home hungry most days. (Young person in Farthing 2012b, p. 19)

Second, depending on the way FSM is delivered in a school, it can be deeply stigmatizing. Poverty is often considered a shameful experience (Lister 2004), and it is understandable that few young people want to be openly identified as poor in front of their classroom peers. However, some ways that FSM are delivered can do exactly that.

Because FSMs have been around, in one shape or form, for over a century, it is popular knowledge across Britain that only poor children get FSM. This means that being identified as receiving FSM is tantamount to being identified as poor. Many schools work to reduce this possibility, by providing discreet, non-identifiable ways of providing young people with credit for their canteens. However, some still use highly visible voucher systems, where young people have to physically collect, carry and hand over their voucher at the canteen till. This can be a highly identifying process, and leaves many children feeling embarrassed and different:

> It was embarrassing, I never wanted to go and get something with people I know in the room. [It makes you feel] like you don't deserve to eat the food. (Young person in Farthing 2012b, p. 24)

This stigma means that many young people choose to go hungry rather than be embarrassed. On any given day, only 83 per cent of students on FSM actually eat the meal they are entitled to (Iniesta-Martinez and Evans 2012, p. 10), and some of this may be due to stigma:

> I do know some of my friends won't get their free lunch, they will wait to get home I think of it was done anonymously then people wouldn't be so nervous about it. (Young people in Farthing 2012b, p. 23)

Thirdly, the only requirement on, and funding provided to, schools is to provide a lunch. As this Education Act (2002, sec.1.6) outlines, FSM 'means food made available for consumption by the pupil as his midday meal on a school day'. No provision is made to provide food at breakfast or in the morning break, or on non-school days. This means that many children go hungry until lunchtime, often 1 or 1.30 in England.

> Getting free school meals doesn't allow me to get any food at break time and sometimes I'm hungry at break and this is difficult. (Young person in Farthing 2012b, p. 18)

This oversight has significant impacts on children's education. Benton and Parker (1998) found that skipping breakfast can decrease recall and memory, and as Sorhaindo and Feinstein (2006) pointed out, adequate blood sugar levels are needed to optimize cognition and learning.

To address this, many English schools offer free or highly subsidized 'breakfast clubs'. These clubs provide healthy, affordable breakfast to pupils; however, unlike the UK's school system, breakfast clubs are not a universal service. While there are no official figures on the number of breakfast clubs, it is estimated that at one point, up to 20,000 clubs existed within schools around England, but as these were voluntary and did not have guaranteed funding, many have closed or face closure since the financial crisis in 2008 (McVeigh 2011). This leads to a sort of 'lottery' when it comes to the ability to access a free or subsidized breakfast. Depending on the school a child attends, they may or may not have access to a breakfast club. Some English children from low income backgrounds can enjoy breakfast, while many others cannot.

Finally, while FSMs are a key nutritional intervention for children on low incomes across the UK, they are obviously limited to days where children attend school. Legally, schools in England are required to operate over 194 days of the year (Education (School Day and School Year) Regulations 1999 (England)), leaving 171 days where low income children do not have access to FSM. This leaves almost half a year of potential hunger.

In short, while the FSM scheme is a long-established and good attempt at improving young people's nutrition for education gains, it is not a silver bullet for the problem of hunger and malnutrition across the UK. It alone does not realize children's right to not go hungry or to an adequate standard of living, and while it goes some way to discharging its responsibility, does not fully meet the government's obligations to provide material assistance in providing nutrition to children in need (Convention on the Rights of the Child, Art. 27).

Various local authorities and various nations (e.g. Scotland and Wales) within the UK have tried different approaches to address these inadequacies. For example, two London councils are currently providing universal FSMs so that all children who attend primary schools in Newham council (Newham 2012) and younger primary school children in Southwark (Southwark 2012) council get free lunches. Scotland has also committed itself to progressively working to extend free provision to nursery and younger primary school students. This partly addresses issues around inadequacy of entitlement, as children from low income but working households would become entitled, and stigma, as eating a free meal would no longer be a marker of poverty.

A detailed review of the impact of providing free school lunchtime meals to all primary school students found that over a two-year period, attainment levels comparable to 4–8 weeks of learning were gained, or approximately 10–21 per cent of a school year, over two years (Brown et al. 2012). Curiously, the same review (Brown et al. 2012) found that when entitlement was extended just to provide free school lunches to children from low income, working households, no measureable effects on attainment were noticed. This perhaps speaks to the value of providing universal services for all; children get the most out of their education when everyone is included.

The Welsh government, on the other hand, has committed itself to extending the provision of breakfast clubs and providing funding to ensure that eventually all schools will have a universally free breakfast club. At one point, half of all Welsh primary schools have a free breakfast club (Welsh Government 2007). This addressed issues around inadequacy of entitlement and provision outside of lunchtime, as well as stigma. No formal evaluation of this breakfast provision has been undertaken. Regardless, it is still perhaps worthwhile noting the Scottish and Welsh approaches, as they are diverging more towards universal provision than the English government appears to be.

Conclusions

Young people living in poor households in the UK often have worse outcomes and experiences within the UK's universal school system. They more frequently obtain poor grades and are less likely to progress on to higher education. While their families make Herculean efforts to ensure that the costs of schooling are met, not all of the additional spends British schools call for can always be made. Children from low income families miss out on school trips, correct uniforms, easy access to computers and the ability to choose the subjects they want to. They often have a more negative time at school, miss more of it and more frequently attend worse schools than their richer peers.

But they also go hungry at school. While the UK has an established and well-developed scheme to provide healthy lunches at school for some young people from families that might otherwise not be able to afford it, this scheme has too many gaps to ensure that no child goes hungry for want of money. Provision for young people from 'working poor' families, before lunchtime and outside of school hours is needed to holistically tackle child hunger in the UK.

While the education system plays a key part in mitigating both hunger and low educational attainment among young people living in poverty, this suggests that there is much potential to improve this role, to realize both children's rights to an adequate standard of living and their right to access education equally.

Understanding education as a humanitarian response requires a focus on ensuring access to an appropriate education for all young people (Brock and McCorriston 2008). The experiences of young people from households living in poverty perhaps speaks to some of the ways in which the UK's seemingly universal education system currently lets marginalized children down. But perhaps more optimistically, addressing the attainment gaps, negative experiences and hunger that these young people spoke about may provide a roadmap for improving British school education into the future.

Questions for reflection

1. Aside from the direct impact of incomes on education as outlined in this chapter, such as the impact of not being able to afford a desk, among others, could there be any indirect relationship between low income and educational attainment? What other mediating factors might help explain this relationship?
2. Alongside measures to reduce poverty, the impact of poverty on young people's education could be reduced by focusing on resilience. That is, enabling young people to do well despite their family incomes. What should be the balance between the two focuses, between poverty reduction and resilience? What sorts of interventions might be required to reduce poverty? What sorts of intervention might be necessary to foster resilience?
3. What could schools and educational facilities do to reduce student hunger? Is this, or should this be, their role?

Further reading

1. Peters et al. 2009. *The Costs of Schooling 2007*. London: Department for Children, Schools and Families.

    Outlines the current costs associated with going to school in England.

2. OECD. 2010. *PISA 2009 Results: Overcoming Social Background – Equity in Learning Opportunities and Outcomes (Volume II)* (online) http://dx.doi.org/10.1787/9789264091504-en (accessed 29 February 2013).

    Outlines the comparative relationship between socio-economic disadvantage and student performance across OECD countries. It explores potential drivers of these inequalities and mechanisms to reduce them.

3. Ridge, T. 2002. 'Experiences and perceptions of school: analysis of the BHPYS data' in *Childhood poverty and social exclusion: from a child's perspective*. Policy Press, Bristol pp. 111–131.

    Ridge's work explores the impact of growing up on a low income in the UK on children, from their perspectives, and this chapter focuses on children's experiences in the classroom.

References

Bellisle, F. (2004). Effects of diet on behaviour and cognition in children. *British Journal of Nutrition*, 92 (2), S227–S232.

Benton, D. (2001). The impact of supply of glucose to the brain on mood and memory. *Nutrition Reviews*, 59(1), S20–S21.

Benton, D. and Parker, P. (1998). Breakfast, blood glucose, and cognition. *American Journal of Clinical Nutrition*, 67(suppl), 772S–778S.

Brock, C. and McCorriston, M. (2008). *Towards the Concept of Education as a Humanitarian Response in the Context of a UNESCO Chair/UNITWIN Network*. London: United Kingdom National Commission for UNESCO.

Brown, V., Crawford, C., Dearden, L., Greaves, E., Kitchen, S., Payne, C., Purdon, S. and Tanner, E. (2012). *Evaluation of the Free School Meals Pilot: Impact Report*. London: Institute of Fiscal Studies.

Clifton, C. and Cook, W. (2012). *A Long Division: Closing the Attainment Gap in England's Secondary Schools*. London: IPPR.

Committee on the Rights of the Child (2008). *Concluding Observations: United Kingdom of Great Britain and Northern Ireland* CRC/C/GBR/CO/4.

CPAG (2012). *Welfare Benefits and Tax Credits Handbook*. London: Child Poverty Action Group.

CPAG, NUT, BYC and KidsCo (2013). *The Cost of Going to School, from Young People's Perspectives*. London: Child Poverty Action Group.

Department for Business Innovation and Skills (2012). *Widening Participation in Higher Education*. London: BIS.

Department for Education (2012a). *Pupil Absence in Schools in England: Autumn Term 2011 and Spring Term 2012*. Available at: http://www.education.gov.uk/rsgateway/DB/SFR/s001090/index.shtml (accessed 5 March 2013).

—— (2012b). *Permanent and Fixed Period Exclusions for Schools in England 2010/11*. Available at: http://www.education.gov.uk/rsgateway/DB/SFR/s001080/index.shtml (accessed 5 March 2013).

—— (2012c). *Schools, Pupils and their Characteristics, January 2012*. Available at: http://www. education.gov.uk/rsgateway/DB/SFR/s001071/index.shtml (accessed 5 March 2013).

—— (2013a). *Attainment Gap at Ages 11, 16 and 19*. Available at: http://www.education.gov.uk/ researchandstatistics/statistics/keystatistics/b00214299/attainment-gap-at-ages-11-16-and-19 (accessed 1 March 2013).

—— (2013b). *School Readiness at Age 5*. Available at: http://www.education.gov.uk/ researchandstatistics/statistics/keystatistics/b00221154/school (accessed 1 March 2013).

Department for Work and Pensions (2012). *Households Below Average Income 2010/2011*. London: DWP.

Farthing, R. (2012a). *Young People's Thoughts on Child Poverty Policy*. London: Child Poverty Action Group.

—— (2012b). *Going Hungry? Young People's Experiences of Free School Meals*. London: Child Poverty Action Group/British Youth Council.

—— (Forthcoming) *Are We Tackling What Matters Most to Young People?: Involving the Targets of Child Poverty Policy in its Creation*. Oxford University: Unpublished doctoral thesis.

Food Statistics Unit (2012). *Family Food 2011*. York: Department for Environment, Food and Rural Affairs.

Foster, B. and Norton, P. (2012). Educational equality for gypsy, roma and traveller children and young people in the UK. *The Equal Rights Review*, 8(suppl), 85–112.

Hogan, G. (2007). *The Impact of Poverty on Young Children's Experience of School*. York: Joseph York Rowntree Foundation.

Iniesta-Martinez, S. and Evans, H. (2012). *Pupils Not Claiming Free School Meals*. Available at: https://www.gov.uk/government/uploads/system/uploads/attachment_data/file/183380/DFE-RR235.pdf (accessed 10 March 2013).

Lister, R. (2004). *Poverty*. London: Polity Press.

London Economics(2008). *Assessing Current and Potential Provision of Free School Meals: Economic Research on Free School Meals Entitlement and Exchequer Costs*. London: London Economics.

McVeigh, T. (2011). Breakfast clubs can rescue a school, but more than half face closure. *The Observer*, Sunday 23rd October 2011,14.

Newham (2012). *Mayors Contract 2012–2013*. London: Newham Council.

OECD (2010). *PISA 2009 Results: Overcoming Social Background – Equity in Learning Opportunities and Outcomes (Volume II)*. Available at: http://dx.doi.org/10.1787/9789264091504-en accessed 29 February 2013.

Ofstead (2012). *The report of Her Majesty's Chief Inspector of Education, Children's Services and Skills: Schools 2011/12*. London: Ofstead.

Peters, M., Carpenter, H., Edwards, G. and Coleman, N. (2009). *The Costs of Schooling 2007*. London: Department for Children, Schools and Families.

Schools Food Trust. (2012). *Primary School Food Survey: School Lunches Vs Packed Lunches, Report Revisited*. Available at: http://www.childrensfoodtrust.org.uk/assets/research-reports/primary_school_lunches_v_packed_lunches_revised2012.pdf (accessed 20 March 2013).

Sorhaindo, A. and Feinstein, L. (2006). *What Is the Relationship Between Child Nutrition and School Outcomes?* London: Centre for Research on the Wider Benefits of Learning.

Southwark (2012). *Thousands More Children Eligible for Free Healthy School Meals from September*. Available at: http://www.southwark.gov.uk/news/article/835/thousands_more_children_eligible_for_free_healthy_school_meals_from_september (accessed 20 March 2013).

Sutton, L., Smith, N., Dearden, C. and Middleton, S. (2007). *A Child's Eye View of Social Difference*. York: Joseph Rowntree Foundation.

Townsend, P. (1979). *Poverty in the United Kingdom: A Survey of Household Resources and Standards*. Los Angeles: University of California Press.

Welsh Government (2007). *600 Breakfast Clubs Now Available in Wales*. Available at: http://wales.gov.uk/topics/educationandskills/learningproviders/schools/foodanddrink/breakfast/freebreakfastspressreleases/600breakfastclubs/?lang=en (accessed 20 March 2013).

Williams, R. and Kaye, M. (2010). *At the End of the Line: Restring the Integrity of the UK's Asylum System*. London: Still Human, Still Here.

World Bank (2010). *World Development Indicators: Education School Enrolment Primary, Net*. Available at: http://data.worldbank.org/indicator (accessed 1 March 2013).

Food Insecurity, Hunger, Nutrition and Education in the USA

Nalini Asha Biggs and Yael Schwarz Freimann

Introduction

While this book offers insight into the very real famine and hunger issues worldwide, this chapter presents a slightly altered understanding of 'education as a humanitarian response to hunger'. Most think of the USA as a land of plenty, yet the disparity between rich and poor grows wider: currently one in five American children experience hunger and food insecurity. Even in the prosperous and resource-rich state of California, children go homeless and experience hunger.

Other issues specific to this economic and social climate are more unusual. There is an epidemic of obesity which also brings nutritional problems and lifelong health issues. Though most Americans are physically close to well-stocked grocery stores, issues of economic inequality, low levels of knowledge about nutrition and poor urban planning have resulted in a significant portion of Americans relying on emergency food supplies.

This chapter reviews these issues across the USA but uses the example of California and Connecticut as a useful case study for many of these complex interactions. First, it provides a brief overview of these issues before summarizing the primary problems faced in America relating to nutrition, hunger and education such as malnutrition, obesity and other related health problems. Second, some of the history and sociology of these complications helps to contextualize these issues. Finally, this chapter reviews some of the latest responses to these issues, summarizing major criticisms of such programmes as 'food stamps', as well as innovative programmes such as school gardens.

Framing this chapter are two vignettes based on ethnographic studies that offer a tangible understanding of the complexities behind hunger and nutrition in the USA. These focus on case studies in California and Connecticut, offering two alternative understandings of the situation. It is nearly impossible to adequately summarize the wide range of issues relating to hunger, nutrition and education in the USA, but these combined approaches provide a broad introduction into these relationships, closing with specific books and articles that might be useful for further reading.

Vignette 1: Education and hunger in San Diego's urban schools

Only a half an hour after the sun has risen, middle school children are lining up outside a school cafeteria, punching in their Personal Identification Numbers (PINs) and making their requests for today's choices in breakfast. A few children sit at the steel picnic tables under the cafeteria's awning, waiting for the bell to strike that calls them to class.

In this part of San Diego there are many such schools noted for their high concentration of 'free or reduced lunch students'. Their numbers are publically listed and selective parents use these statistics to make choices about where to settle their families, with these regions being considered undesirable. Still, even in the most affluent neighbourhoods there are students in public schools who qualify for 'free or reduced lunch' because of their parents' low income.

Each morning and at lunch I took turns with my co-teachers standing at the cafeteria's windowed counter because my students, having multiple disabilities, often needed extra assistance remembering their PINs or manipulating the digital keypad. Like all other students, I helped with ensuring daily nutrition and food choice but for Special Education teachers this activity often takes on additional importance. People with disabilities are disproportionally more likely to have low income and rely on government assistance to get enough food and other basic needs.

Even those students who came from more affluent families still accessed their breakfasts and lunches in the same way, using a PIN to pay for meals which was linked to a pre-paid account. It was still clear, however, who had this luxury because these students were able to choose the 'a la carte' options such as nachos and pizza rather than the nutritionally circumscribed offerings of the day.

'Nutrition education' rarely stayed within the confines of a Science classroom: teachers in schools with higher numbers of free and reduced lunches had to consider the daily nutritional and health needs of the students both at the time and in their futures.

In an area of San Diego where 'drive-by shootings' were not uncommon, our students felt liberated, rather than restrained, by their school uniforms because they masked the relatively impoverished homes from which they came. In addition to this wider context, students with severe disabilities were much more likely to be neglected, making our jobs sometimes overlapping with social services. 'Neglect' more often meant malnourishment and even starvation for students using wheelchairs and having limited communication. In the previous year at this school, one boy had died of starvation and his parents were on trial for manslaughter.

This is the reality for many educators in the USA especially in urban areas or the many parts of rural America where most families live near or below the poverty line. While I worked in California, known as America's breadbasket and the world's eighth largest economy, my colleagues and I fought against hunger and even starvation every day.

Overview of food insecurity, nutrition and education in the USA

While one of the most basic human needs is food, even in developed, wealthy countries like the United States, food security is a real problem. In these contexts it manifests less as famine or rampant starvation but rather as an inability for families to access sufficient food or nutrition. Here the definition of food security takes on a more relative meaning. Rather than droughts or widespread severe poverty of entire geographic contexts, the ability to acquire acceptable foods in socially acceptable ways, without resorting to emergency food supplies is limited for specific families and small pockets within cities and rural counties.

The top 10 per cent of America's wealthy families often live only a few miles away from those families who are a part of the 15 per cent of US households that experience food insecurity. According to the US Department of Agriculture's Economic Research Service's annual study, 1 in 6 Americans is food insecure and 1 in 4 children live in a food-insecure household. This rate is increasing and while there have been significant efforts to curb this problem, it remains a very real issue for researchers, policy makers and practitioners nationwide.

Food insecurity and its causes

Although a food-rich country, not all Americans have equal access to this food or to adequate nutrition. The US Department of Agriculture's Economic Research Service's annual study measuring food security in the United States shows that nearly '31 million Americans ... still face hunger as a regular fact of life' (U.S. Department of Agriculture. 2008). In addition to chronic food insecurity, many more are 'at risk' (Bickel et al. 2000). Both public and private initiatives attempt to mitigate these varied risks through more immediate means such as providing actual food stuffs as well as more distal methods such as education on social security programmes and nutrition.

These programmes, though increasingly popular, are losing funding. The percentage of Americans living near or below the poverty line has increased in the past two decades to 37 million or 12.7 per cent of the population (US Department of Health and Human Services 2003), and there are currently over 25 million Americans on food stamps (Economic Research Service 2005).

The American Dietetic Association has argued that this recent reduction in funding has 'negatively impacted domestic food and nutrition security' (2006, p. 1). When cuts have been made to related forms of welfare, Cook et al. (2002) found that children were more likely to visit the hospital and the emergency room as compared to children whose benefits were not reduced. Immigrants feel these impacts at a higher rate than others, with food insecurity being four times as likely amongst the families of Latino farm workers who move with the seasonal crops around the country (Capps et al. 2002; Quandt et al. 2004; Van Hook and Balistreri 2006).

Research has shown, therefore, that in order to reduce food insecurity there must be a wider range of support programmes than those that simply focus on immediate access to food, such as food stamp programmes and food banks. Other distal issues are highly correlated with food insecurity, especially in the more vulnerable populations, such as unemployment and underemployment, the high cost of housing in much of the USA, the high cost of medical care and difficulty navigating government-supported medical care, drug abuse, mental health issues, the high cost of childcare and the consistent reduction of public funding (US Conference of Mayors 2005).

The US context for food insecurity is also marked by ethnic disparities. Around one in five Latino families are food insecure (Nord et al. 2007). African Americans are roughly 13 per cent of the general population, yet they account for 38 per cent of those who access food banks. While overall there are higher numbers of families with food insecurity living in urban areas, rural areas have a higher concentration with more persistent poverty and more female-headed families (USDA Economic Research Service 2005).

Lack of food in the USA is not the issue causing food insecurity. While supermarkets might always be teeming with options, pocketbooks might be bare, transportation problematic or options in certain neighbourhoods may be limited.

Healthy food in the USA is expensive. Fresh vegetables, fruits and multi-grains are much more costly than high-sugar, high-fat processed and canned foods. The same is true for high quality protein, with leaner meats being more expensive. White bread, pasta, and canned goods are much more affordable; they also have a longer shelf life so the initial investment seems more worthwhile.

Geography can also cause access issues. Urban centres often lack supermarkets and inhabitants with no mode of transportation are confined to the corner stores in the area, which are often pricey and carry limited selection. In cities that have good public transportation this is less of an issue, but many cities in the USA have inefficient or negligible public transportation systems, making it difficult to access quality food.

In areas where there are higher concentrations of families using these services, many stores will display signs that they accept food stamps. While there are also assistance programmes for emergency situations such as hurricanes and floods, most hunger-related programmes focus on the immediate nutritional needs rather than responding to the complex cycles of poverty and inequality found in the USA.

Yet research has shown repeatedly that there is a large segment of the population living in fragile conditions that make them susceptible to hunger and housing insecurity. Though they live in an otherwise prosperous country, many families experience the subsistence level conditions of developing countries, and many of the health issues that come with these conditions.

This vulnerability is intimately linked to related factors that have little to do with physical proximity to food or making conscious, informed decisions about nutrition. Yet the 'accepted' framework is criticized for focusing on providing immediate meals rather than tackling the more complex cultural, economic, social and even environmental issues creating these conditions.

Responses to food insecurity

The kinds of programmes intended to respond to these issues are supported by both public and private institutions and often include a range of services such as the WIC (Women, Infants and Children) Programme that offers related education and support for this population. Other programmes target nutrition and food more specifically such as SNAP (Supplemental Nutrition Assistance Program) which is more commonly known as 'food stamps', allowing individuals earning low income to purchase food in most stores. This kind of programme attempts to respond to chronic food insecurity because it requires somewhat long-term documentation of low income and other factors.

Emergency food responses aim to address food insecurity that is less chronic and more intermittent, yet they often take the place of programmes such as SNAP because of the lack of education about eligibility and the stigma associated with welfare.

Food banks, sometimes called food pantries and food shelves, are forms of emergency food supplies, most commonly supported by local non-profits and religious organizations. Anyone can walk in, off the street, and ask for a grocery bag full of common food items such as bread and canned goods. These are more frequently visited by families who intermittently find themselves without the ability to purchase food, either because they have run out of food stamps, cash or credit.

Soup kitchens are similar but only supply a single meal at a time and are more active during winter holidays. These are more commonly visited by homeless or housing-insecure families and single males. Similar programmes are set up in the wake of major disasters and are publically funded when a situation designated as a federal disaster arises, such as was Hurricane Katrina.

Finally, and most relevant to this chapter, are the school lunch programmes. Though labelled lunch, they often include breakfast and even after-school snacks in some schools. The parameters for eligibility for these programmes are much broader than for other government assistance with far more children receiving these meals than participating in food stamps. School meals are also regulated based on current Food and Drug Administration (FDA) nutritional guidelines, which change according to research and practice. These same guidelines are used in nutritional education, which most recently changed from using a food pyramid illustration, ubiquitous in public school cafeterias across the country, to an image of a plate of food with portions of different kinds of food appropriate to their guidelines.

Because of the strong relationship between the FDA and school lunch programmes, American culture is shaped, in part, by these guidelines, with the former 'food pyramid' nutritional guide being incorporated into popular culture.

Any of these programmes that receive public funds also record and track data on their participants, largely to maintain access to these funds that require participation by individuals who have been identified as low-income. The same income levels are used to qualify individuals for other public assistance such as healthcare.

Privately funded programmes also track participants, sometimes offering a more accurate illustration of food insecurity in the USA because these participants are not limited by rates of taxable income and can include illegal aliens and those not receiving government assistance but who are still food insecure. The 2006 *Hunger in America* study completed by a national network of food banks found that food insecurity has risen in the past ten years, even correcting for population inflation. Food banks tended to be visited by families that represented a gray area between the extreme poor relying on food stamps and those families who have low incomes and while being at risk, do not chronically experience hunger.

It is important to note these gray areas because such markers as the poverty line or participation in the Food Stamp Programme are not necessarily good indicators for food insecurity. It is estimated that only half of those Americans who are eligible have actually enrolled in the Food Stamp Program, with two-thirds of those families who believe they are not eligible being in fact eligible (O'Brien and Aldeen 2007).

Only about one-third of families who access some form of emergency food assistance such as food banks are concurrently using food stamps even if they are eligible and a third have never applied for this programme at any time in the past. Only about half of emergency food recipients have been accessing some form of food-related government assistance, including WIC and school lunch (ibid.). In this sense, some of the private responses to food insecurity have highlighted the limitations of the more systematic government responses.

Clearly, there are complexities to responding to food insecurity both at the emergency and chronic levels. In order to illustrate these relationships, the following vignette describes one food pantry which supplies to a community in Connecticut.

Vignette 2: Making healthy choices in 'food deserts'

Founded in 1972 with the specific aim of helping hungry children, this food pantry has grown to include all segments of the population and now distributes clothing as well. It is set in the heart of Hartford, easily accessible by bus and surrounded by some of the city's poorest neighbourhoods. This pantry operates entirely on donations and receives no government help. Families receive two days' worth of groceries based on family size.

The pantry can serve 150 adults and 350 children a week but recently they have had to turn away individuals because there simply wasn't enough. The same people come back week after week for food. The dedicated staff has watched the children growing up and some now come in with their own children.

While the pantry is busy, it's mostly with women and children and there are very few men present. It's clear at first glance that no one is starving, as many waiting to be served are actually overweight.

Of these clients, 70 per cent come in weekly and while they also visit the corner store, this is where they get most of their food supply. Some visit other pantries as well. They tell me it's mostly because of the cost of living, rent in particular.

> I can't get rent for free … [g]otta cut somewhere and coming here saves me at least fifty dollars a week. [Without the pantry] I guess I'd wait for McDonald' to throw out their food for the day. It's not used you know; it's still good.

For the past few years I have been working with local food pantries like this one in the mid-size city of Hartford, Connecticut. I consult with managers and visit the homes of clients, trying to learn what works and where we can adjust our practices to help more families get the nutrition they need. We have one of the highest concentrations of extremely low-income families living on the outskirts of the suburbs where most of the grocery stores, offering a range of fresh produce and other products, are centralized.

While other cities benefit from efficient and low-cost public transportation, the town feels much larger than it truly is, especially during winter with limited transport service offering access for these urban poor. The result is a large gap between those who can access these relative luxuries and those visiting these food pantries, sometimes called food banks.

The families I worked with went to great lengths to keep low-paying jobs in the suburbs and spent much of their day travelling to and from employment that still barely covered their living expenses. For a single mother with several children, after a long day's commute and labour, the last thing she wants to do is commute further to a large grocery store only to return home to prepare a comparatively labour-intensive meal when the alternative is a similarly priced or less expensive meal from a fast food restaurant.

Many of the people I met did not have proper storage in their homes, oftentimes neither did the food pantries, making fresh fruit and vegetables a difficult option even when technically available. While occasionally some parents made an effort to make conscious nutritional decisions when shopping, overall there was a serious lack of knowledge about nutritional qualities of foods and information provided on the packages was frequently ignored.

The needs of children are often different than their parents' and guardians', something the pantry staff take into consideration. The steady stream of regulars at the food pantry made one church group that volunteered realize that many of these families were hungry on the weekends because their kids were no longer getting lunches through their school. The group then decided to create a programme that provides backpacks full of food for the families of school-age children to take home over the weekend.

> We have constant interaction with these people. We want to know what needs are out there so we can try to meet them as a community.

At one pantry, usage went up 180 per cent since 2008, when the recession hit.

> We're seeing such a huge increase in the need for assistance. It's a constant slew of new faces.... We are really set up as an emergency food pantry, we're here for those times when lack of school lunches leave parents with higher food bills or there is some unforeseen situation. We are set up to supplement, not provide.

Most users questioned had never been to a food pantry before.

> I never thought I'd have to come here but it was food or having my kid participate in soccer. It sounds trivial but I couldn't say no.

The North End of Hartford is known for being a very poor area, riddled with crime. Shootings, gang fights and drug deals are common occurrences. In the month of August 2010, three victims were shot 10 minutes apart at different corner stores by separate, unrelated, drive-by shooters. One victim, shot in the stomach, was five months pregnant. Staff in a church-hosted food bank find the situation dire.

Single moms make up a large portion of recipients and many have become volunteers to get first pick at the pantry.

> I never knew if I would get food – now that I volunteer here I know I will. We need to get through the day – that's our main concern. Keeping our kids off the street, feeding them, staying alive. This service helps. But it's going to take a lot more than food to fix our mess.

stated one client/volunteer with three young children at home and a boyfriend in jail.

Relationships between education, hunger and malnutrition

It is clear that food insecurity is a real problem for a significant portion of Americans and different kinds of programmes attempt to respond to this issue. Some of these responses are educational: people need to know which programmes are available in order to access them.

However, most educationalists interested in hunger and nutrition in the USA tend to explore the impact of hunger and malnutrition on educational outcomes of children. Public education includes nutritional education at several levels across different disciplines. Each state has different educational standards but in general students learn about basic nutrition and health in Science and Physical Education.

It is difficult to extrapolate to what degree this education works because of the many external factors on nutrition. What is easier to capture is how hunger and malnutrition impact children and their education. School lunch programmes are, of course, one of the ways public education has attempted to respond to these issues. In order to preface some of the other responses to hunger and malnutrition, it is useful to review the other ways hunger and malnutrition impact children and families.

Homelessness and housing insecurity impact children far more than most might imagine in the USA. Joy, et al. (1994) found that over 70 per cent of people seeking emergency food were members of families with children and though 84 per cent were living below the poverty line (with 20 per cent having no income at all), the large majority were not enrolled in the Food Stamp Program. While the more visible homeless populations are often men, the average homeless family is more likely to be a single mother with two young children. These kinds of statistics highlight the importance of noting the difference between populations that are consistently requiring and using food stamp programmes and those who are at risk and could benefit from education on these programmes.

Researchers have attempted to pinpoint which aspects of poverty and food insecurity have the most direct impact on children's health and education, especially since recent congressional funding cuts. Fuller et al. (2002) found that food insecurity in a family had a strong impact on whether or not mothers read books to their children. It also impacted rates of maternal depression. These results of food insecurity in turn impacted rates of aggressive behaviour in children and inattentiveness. Those mothers who had higher incomes were able to read to their children more often and were able to maintain stable emotional well-being, which had a direct impact on child development and schooling experience.

Studies have shown that these populations accessing emergency food are consistently malnourished. Children who are homeless have diets low in dairy products, fruits and vegetables and breads and cereals (Taylor and Koblinsky 1994). Children such as these often have low rates of immunizations and related health problems causing higher rates of hospitalization (Alperstein et al. 1988). Mothers tend to have calcium deficiency in particular in addition to other nutritional deficiencies.

Education is shaped by this context in both formal education (school-based or organizes classes for adults) as well as informal education (social workers or other practitioners offering information).

Teachers in these contexts are well versed in child protective services (CPS) and often act as mediators between families and government services. In the urban pockets of low income and high population density, the informal education through interaction between school nurses and children and their families is more likely to include the medical complications of teenage pregnancies, untreated infections, drug and alcohol addiction, abuse and neglect. It is not uncommon for Special Education classrooms to include children labelled as 'crack babies', whose intellectual disability was directly linked to the use of crack cocaine during pregnancy. Because of long-term drug addiction problems in the families of these children, malnutrition, hunger and neglect are also a concurrent issue, often exacerbating the disability.

In short, public education is marked by the residual effects of low nutrition and hunger in these inner city schools as well as low-income, rural counties. Public schools are often the primary connection families have with social services, and educational professionals remain the first 'line of defence' against the health problems that result from hunger and malnutrition.

Schools, nutrition education and obesity

America has grown to become known as the 'fat' country. While this reflects the stereotype of American consumerism and excess, it is also representative of deeper socio-economic inequalities. Obesity is largely a problem of the poor, with much higher rates in parts of the country with the lowest income and other resources.

Some, like Beebout (2002), argue that obesity is the biggest nutritional issue in the USA, far beyond hunger issues. Over 1 in 10 American children are obese, which is defined as having high body mass indexes (BMIs). Even more fall within risky BMI levels. This is much higher within certain ethnic groups, which are reviewed in later sections.

One case study of a food pantry funded by a faith-based organization (FBO) in California found that most of the people accessing these services were overweight or obese. Causes for this obesity are complex, from both nutritional and medical issues to cultural associations with different kinds of food and food practices. Just under a third of Californians with low incomes are in fact obese (Rendon 2011).

Aside from the medical and social impacts, it is also financially more sustainable to fund anti-obesity efforts now rather than face the expensive costs later. Efforts to normalize weight by as little as 5–10 per cent will save California, for example, between $6 and $13 billion over five years (Chenoweth 2005).

Potential solutions: Food stamps redefined

In the USA, the Food Stamp Programme (FSP) was recently renamed the Supplemental Nutrition Assistance Programme or SNAP in 2008. While there are many responses to food insecurity and hunger, this is by far the largest and most comprehensive federal program, administered by the FDA. Because it is so large and pervasive it also has come under the most scrutiny as 'welfare' and for its occasional abuse by some participants.

Because over 33 million Americans have signed up for SNAP, made eligible by a combination of family size and income, it is also used as a marker and data collection source for several indicators of nutrition, health, income and employment and other demographics.

Researchers and practitioners continue to attempt to improve this widespread programme because of its many shortcomings. SNAP serves a narrow portion of the population who were aware of them, who have qualified for them and who have completed the requisite paperwork. Many who need these programmes fail one or more of these prerequisites, with awareness and education on the process of application being one of the major obstacles.

While the amount of money provided each month is supposed to feed the family adequately, a large portion of those receiving food stamps supplement their meals with emergency food or go hungry because it is not enough. It is unclear to what extent this is due to poor choices in food selection or an inaccurate assessment of cost by the FDA for different contexts.

The FSP is often widely criticized because of the large range of choices offered to the individual. Food stamps may be used to purchase any food products regardless of nutritional value. While this is a federal program, states have some choice in how the implement this support, especially in terms of how the educational component of SNAP is implemented and evaluated. In California's implementation, about 80 per cent of food stamp offices featured a resource kit that exposed recipients to nutritional and health education periodically. For many families, food stamps are the only interaction with the government in terms of health and nutrition, so these office visits have taken a central role in spreading related education to a much wider population than for other programmes such as Women, Infant, and Child (WIC) or disability assistance (Ghirardelli et al. 2011).

While food stamps were simply handed out in the past, like ration cards, now the programme has been reframed as a method for implementing a widespread educational intervention. These offices provide pamphlets and posters in different languages to these parents as they wait to receive their aid. This information focuses on how to seek out, purchase and prepare low-cost, nutritious meals, as well as including education on exercise (Ghirardelli et al. 2011).

As with any widespread and popular federal program, SNAP requires improvement, especially in order to serve the diverse population of the USA. Its constant evolution reflects the awareness policy makers have of these kinds of innovative models, and local adaptations of this programme allow for pilot programmes to evaluate new methods.

Potential solutions: Experiments with garden-based education

California makes for a useful case study of both the many challenges educators face and new possibilities in nutrition education. The favourable climate offers year-round sunshine and temperate weather for schools to cultivate small gardens on campus and use the activities to learn about mathematics, science, health and a range of other subjects. Charter schools in particular have made use of this opportunity though large, public schools have been encouraged to open their own gardens.

In 1995, the California Department of Education (CDE) launched the 'A Garden in Every School' initiative (Assembly Bill 1014) and in 2006 the California Instructional School Garden Programme (CISGP) was passed, providing 15 million US dollars for grants to promote, develop and sustain instructional school gardens for three years (2007–2009).

These gardens represent more than simply outdoor venues for academic discussions. Children are especially vulnerable to vitamin deficiencies and with the average school-aged child eating half or less than the recommended servings of fruits and vegetables, educators have ample motivation to encourage positive interactions with the avocados and oranges that grow so well in this climate (Vadiveloo et al. 2009). While most of the research shows that even when accessible, children simply choose other foods, the experiences of some Californian educators prove otherwise.

Children who participate in these interventions have shown an increased preference for and consumption of fruits and vegetables (Parmer et al. 2009; Heim et al. 2009; Morris and Zidenberg-Cherr 2002; Morgan et al. 2010; Hermann et al. 2006; McAleese and Rankin 2007; Somerset and Markwell 2009). Yet, because these initiatives are new, little more is known about what contributes to their success and the long-term effects of this education.

Evaluations of how schools access funding and set up their gardens showed that small charter schools were more likely to take advantage of this opportunity and it was extremely valuable to have a designated educator already present within the school community who could personally take on this responsibility (Hazzard et al. 2012). Otherwise administrators felt that while this was a worthwhile endeavour it might not be sustainable without individual teacher support. Most schools also felt that even smaller grants would have been sought out.

Potential solutions: Community investment

Community gardens, school gardens and local farmers' markets in urban centres are all effective ways to engage the local population while providing access to healthy foods. Such community participation has the potential for sharp reduction in poverty if the poor can become an active and vocal part of the processes (Chambers 2007).

The recent trend of local growth restaurants that support local farms or community gardens has been viewed as both socially responsible and aesthetically desirable by local populations. These restaurants attempt to support local growers (both commercial and hobbyists) as well as hire and train locals on the kinds of products and methods required for their menus. These restaurants provide job training in conjunction with healthy food options that reduce the 'carbon footprint' in addition to increasing the diversity of produce available.

In Hartford, Connecticut, *The Kitchen Cafe – Food for Good* also runs cooking classes for the community and provides culinary training. This specific programme has been successful in recruiting local youth – who might otherwise be lured into gang-related activities during these unstructured, unsupervised times – into after-school programmes.

Integrating the local, economic and cultural needs of the community has long been a goal for organizations because this increases the sustainability of programmes. They are often complex to fund and require extremely dedicated personnel to start up, but after this kind of organic integration into local needs, these programmes have a higher rate of return in terms of both involvement and economic sustainability.

How community programmes like these are evaluated also shapes what we call success and how subsequent educational efforts might be modified. Gerstein et al. (2010) experimented with learner-centered nutrition education with Latina mothers to promote the use of fruits and vegetables in daily diets in California. These researchers found that the women preferred an educational environment that was open, allowing for conversation between participants rather than educator-centered and traditional education. In particular the nutritional education was immediately meaningful because this structure allowed participants to relate the theoretical concepts to their daily lives.

> This finding is remarkable given the classes' short duration (15–20 minutes) and the number of months (4–6) since they had attended the class. Intervention participants reported remembering opportunities to interact with other participants in the class and remembering a perceived emotional safety in the class setting.

These kinds of programmes have been shown to effectively support public assistance programmes such as food stamps (Allen 1999). The combined impact of both food and new jobs addresses the issue of food security more completely than other programmes and because they require community support, they are often more sustainable and less likely to be cut due to lack of popularity (Kantor 2001). When these programmes are integrated into school meal programmes, they become especially productive, making school lunches more palatable, sustainable and economically viable.

Conclusion

It is difficult to accurately summarize within one chapter the wide array of relationships between education and hunger/nutrition in the USA. This is primarily because the USA is itself an extremely heterogeneous country and even within states there are a multitude of ecological factors impacting nutrition and education.

In order to better understand the kinds of responses to hunger and nutrition issues in the USA, it is helpful to take into consideration the causes of food insecurity, a term used to describe the range of experiences of hunger, malnutrition and food shortages, both potential and real.

The most direct of these causes is low income, which in the USA can be quite relative given different geographies and family needs. Many of the predictors for low income in the USA, such as ethnicity, education, gender and ability, are also predictors for food insecurity. Furthermore, responses to food insecurity are often inclusive of both intermittent and chronic needs. For many in the USA, simply being employed, some education and housing might not ensure food security. The abrupt loss of employment, sudden illness or death or even the addition of a new member to the household is often the trigger event that places many American families into food insecurity.

The results of food insecurity are as varied as its causes. Children face developmental issues with low nutrition or the low nutrition of pregnant mothers. Children show higher rates of hyperactivity and lower levels of school achievement when faced with food insecurity within their families, even if they themselves have not experienced hunger.

Both public and private responses to food insecurity have attempted to not only meet the immediate needs of food insecurity but also alter the underlying causes. However, these are often criticized for not doing enough, especially to break the cycle of poverty, but rather rely on volunteers and charity to meet immediate needs. Emergency food supplies are common among local charities, especially in the form of food banks.

A vignette of one such bank, located in Connecticut, reveals the complex situation most participants experience. This window into American life reveals the choices many must make in order to avoid hunger, which are often based on day-to-day difficulties of geography and economics. Their reactions to these services show that simply providing the economic access to food sources will not entirely solve the problem of food insecurity in the USA. Rather, other more innovative measures have been explored to hopefully meet these needs in the diverse ways that each community requires.

One of the potential solutions is that of school gardens which serve to provide fresh fruits and vegetables to children while also providing much needed nutritional education. These pilot programmes have been successful in California, where the climate is supportive.

In other areas such as the East Coast of the country, community gardens are gaining support by restaurants bringing economic opportunities for locals as well as fresh foods. Finally, food stamp programmes are ever-changing because of the high level of public scrutiny of welfare programmes. Some projects are integrating nutritional education with these programmes in different ways, hoping to better understand what works for higher risk populations such as single mothers.

While poverty rates are increasing in the USA with food insecurity an ever-present threat, there has been progress in which interventions work for different kinds of communities and populations. Those researchers, policy makers and practitioners interested in education, hunger and nutrition in the USA must constantly attempt the difficult balance between reaching as many Americans with a standard level of consideration and allowing local actors the freedom to adapt each intervention for their own specific needs.

Food insecurity in the United States manifests itself as obesity and malnourishment due to poor food options. Lack of access to healthy foods, lack of education and lack of financial resources have all led to this situation. What role can education play in creating a more sustainable food ecosystem? Currently, schools serve to provide food for those that qualify for free or reduced-rate breakfast and lunch. Programmes that focus more on nutrition education and less on handouts would be beneficial. Great success has been evident in models where nutrition education plays a key role. It is as simple as the old adage – give a man a fish and he eats for a day, teach a man to fish and you feed him for a lifetime.

Questions for reflection

1. What are some common barriers to food security for poor Americans living in urban settings? How are these different from food security issues of those living in less-affluent countries?
2. In what ways do teachers interact with nutritional and food security issues in the USA?
3. Discuss the relative sustainability of different strategies presented in this chapter: how do programmes such as food pantries compare with community and school gardens or food stamp programmes in different countries as compared with the USA?

Further reading

1. Poppendieck, J. (2011) *Free for All: Fixing School Food in America*. CA: University of California Press.

   Offers an accessible yet exceptionally well-cited account of not only the main struggles faced in America's schools but also the complexities of their responses. Several journal articles also summarize the major issues introduced by this chapter.

2. Casey et al. (2006). The association of child and household food insecurity with childhood overweight status. *Pediatrics, 118*(5), e1406–e1413.

   Provides greater detail on the relationships between poverty, food insecurity, obesity and other issues in the USA.

3. Guthrie, J. F., Stommes, E. and Voichick, J. (2006). Evaluating food stamp nutrition education: Issues and opportunities. *Journal of Nutrition Education and Behavior, 38*(1), 6–11.

   Offers an introduction to the issues around food stamps and education in the USA, which is one of the most hotly debated political issues related to this area of study.

4. Himmelgreen, DA. and Romero-Daza, N. (2010). Eliminating 'Hunger' in the U.S.: Changes in policy regarding the measurement of food security. *Food and Foodways, 18*(1–2), 96–113.

   As this topic is highly politicized within the US context, this reference discusses the recent ramifications on research practices.

References

Allen, P. (1999). Reweaving the food security safety net: Mediating entitlement and entrepreneurship. *Agriculture and Human Values, 16*(2), 117–129.

Alperstein, G., Rappaport, C. and Flanigan, J. M. (1988). Health problems of homeless children in New York City. *American Journal of Public Health, 78*(9), 1232–1233.

Beebout, H. (2002). Nutrition, food security and obesity. *Family Well-Being after Welfare Reform*, March, pp. 10–25.

Bickel, G., Nord, M., Price, C., Hamilton, W. and Cook, J. (2000). *Guide to Measuring Household Food Security, Revised*. Alexandria, VA: US Department of Agriculture, Food and Nutrition Service.

Capps, R., Ku, L. and Fix, M. (2002). *How Are Immigrants Faring after Welfare Reform? Preliminary Evidence from Los Angeles and New York City*. Office of the Assistant Secretary for Planning and Evaluation: US Department of Health and Human Services.

Chambers, R. (2007). Participation and poverty. *Palgrave Macmillan Journals, 50*(2), 20–28.

Chenoweth, D. (2005). *The Economic Costs of Physical Inactivity, Obesity, and Overweight in California Adults: Health Care, Workers Compensation, and Lost Productivity*. Sacramento, CA: California Department of Health Services (Cancer Prevention and Nutrition Section).

Cook, J. T., Frank, D. A., Berkowitz, C., Balck, M. M., Casey, P. H., Cutts, D. B., Meyers, A. F., Zaldivar, N., Skalicky, A., Levenson, S. and Heeren, T. (2002). Welfare reform and the health of young children. *Archives of Pediatrics and Adolescent Medicine, 156*(7), 678–684.

Economic Research Service. (2005). *Food Security in the United States: Household Survey Tools.* Washington D.C.: United State Department of Agriculture (USDA).".

Fuller, B., Caspary, G., Kagan, S. L., Gauthier, C., Huang, D., Carroll, J. and McCarthy, J. (2002). Does maternal employment influence poor children's social development? *Early Child Research Quarterly, 17*(4), 470–497.

Gerstein, D., Martin, A., Crocker, N., Reed, H., Elfant, M., and Crawford, P. (2010). Using learner-centered education to improve fruit and vegetable intake in California WIC participants. *Journal of Nutrition Education and Behavior, 42*(4), 216–224.

Ghirardelli, A., Linares, A. and Fong, A. (2011). Usage and recall of the food stamp office resource kit (FSORK) by food stamp applicants in 4 California counties. *Journal of Nutrition Education and Behavior, 43*(S2), S86–S95.

Hazzard, E., Moreno, E., and Beall, D. (2012). Factors contributing to a school's decision to apply for the California instructional school garden program. *Journal of Nutrition Education and Behavior, 3*(4), 1–5.

Heim, S., Stang,J., and Ireland, M. (2009). A garden pilot project enhances fruit and vegetable consumption among children. *Journal of the American Dietetic Association, 109*(7), 1220–1226.

Hermann, J. et al. (2006). After-school gardening improves children's reported vegetable intake and physical activity. *Journal of Nutrition Education and Behavior, 38*(3), 201–202.

Joy, A. et al. (1994). Hunger in California: What interventions are needed? *Journal of the American Dietetic Association, 94*(7), 749–752.

Kantor, L. S. (2001). Community food security programs improve food access. *Food Review, 24*(1), 20–26.

Lee, R., Cubbin, C. (2002). Neighborhood context and youth cardiovascular health behaviors. *American Journal of Public Health, 92*(3), 428–436.

McAleese, J. and Rankin, L. (2007). Garden-based nutrition education affects fruit and vegetable consumption in sixth-grade adolescents. *Journal of the American Dietician Association, 107*(4), 662–665.

Morgan, P. et al. (2010). The impact of nutrition education with and without a school garden on knowledge, vegetable intake and preferences and quality of school life among primary-school students. *Public Health and Nutrition, 13*(11), 1931–1940.

Morris, J. and Zidenberg-Cherr, S. (2002). Garden-enhanced nutrition curriculum improves fourth-grade school children's knowledge of nutrition and preferences for some vegetables. *Journal of the American Dietetic Association, 102*(1), 91–93.

——— (2007). *Household Food Security in the United States*, US Department of Agriculture, Economic Research Service, ERR–66.

O'Brien, D. and Aldeen, H. (2007). *Hunger in America: The Nation's Food Bank Network Fourth National Hunger Study 2006.* Chicago: America's Second Harvest – The Nation's Food Bank Network.

Parmer, S., Salisbury-Glennon, J., Shannon, D. and Struempler, B. (2009). School gardens: an experiential learning approach for a nutrition education program to increase fruit and vegetable knowledge, preference, and consumption among second-grade students. *Journal of Nutrition Education and Behavior, 41*(3), 212–217.

Poppendieck, J. (1998). *Sweet Charity? Emergency Food and the End of Entitlement.* New York, NY: Viking Press, 368 pp.

Quandt, S. A., Arcury, T. A., Early, J., Tapia, J. and Davis, J. D. (2004). Household food security among migrant and seasonal Latino farmworkers in North Carolina. *Public Health Reports, 119*(6), 568–576.

Rendon, C. (2011). Food pantries, poverty, and social justice. *El Nuevo Sol,* 33–40.

Somerset, S. and Markwell, K. (2009). Impact of a school-based food garden on attitudes and identification skills regarding vegetables and fruit: a 12-month intervention trial. *Public Health Nutrition, 12*(2), 214–221.

Taylor, M. and Koblinsky, S. (1994). Food consumption and eating behavior of homeless preschool children. *Journal of Nutrition Education, 26*(1), 20–25.

The American Dietetic Association. (2006). Position of the American dietetic association: Food insecurity and hunger in the United States. *Journal of the American Dietetic Association, 106*(3), 446–458.

US Conference of Mayors. (2005). Sodexho Hunger and Homelessness Survey, 2004.

U.S. Department of Agriculture, Household Food Security in the United States. (2008). Available at: http://www.fns.usda.gov/pd/fssummar.htm. Accessed 21 July 2010.

US Department of Health and Human Services. (2003). Indicators of Welfare Dependence: Annual Report to Congress.

USDA Economic Research Service. (2005). Rural Poverty At A Glance.

Vadiveloo, M., Zhu, L. and Quatromoni, P. (2009). Diet and physical activity patterns of school-aged children. *Journal of the American Dietetic Association, 109*(1), 145–151.

Van Hook, J. and Balistreri, K. S. (2006). Ineligible parents, eligible children: Food stamps receipt, allotments, and food insecurity among children of immigrants. *Social Science Research, 35*(1), 228–251.

Index